Red Arrows
in Camera

Red

Arrows
in Camera

Keith Wilson

First published in 2012

A catalogue record for this book is available from the British Library

ISBN 978 0 85733 154 0

Library of Congress control no. 2011946140

Published by Haynes Publishing, Sparkford, Yeovil, Somerset BA22 7JJ, UK
Tel: 01963 442030 Fax: 01963 440001
Int. tel: +44 1963 442030 Int. fax: +44 1963 440001
E-mail: sales@haynes.co.uk
Website: www.haynes.co.uk

Haynes North America Inc.
861 Lawrence Drive, Newbury Park,
California 91320, USA

Printed in the USA by Odcombe Press LP,
1299 Bridgestone Parkway, La Vergne, TN 37086

Credits
Project Manager: Sophie Blackman and Jonathan Falconer
Copy editor: Jane Hutchings
Page design: Rod Teasdale
Proofreader: Dave Rankin
Indexer: Dean Rockett

Royal Air Force
Benevolent Fund
THE HEART OF THE RAF FAMILY

In memory of Flt Lt Jon Egging
and Flt Lt Sean Cunningham
50p from the sale of this book will be
donated to the RAF Benevolent Fund
Registered charity 1081009 and SC038109

Contents

Foreword

E. J. Van Koningsveld

The Royal Air Force of today is a very different force to the one that existed at its conception over 90 years ago. Since its formation in 1918, it has seen the development of aircraft progress from the elementary flying machines of the Great War, through the early jet age of the 1940s, the Cold War era of the '50s to '80s to the modern fighting machines of the present day. But while the RAF has constantly evolved and adapted, one thing remains unchanged; the quality, professionalism and dedication of its people. These qualities enable the RAF to remain a flexible and agile force and are exactly those that the Royal Air Force Aerobatic Team (RAFAT) – the Red Arrows – exists to promote.

Regarded as the finest aerobatic team in the world, the Red Arrows are the epitome of brilliance – as reflected in their motto 'Éclat'. Tasked not only with showcasing the excellence and professionalism of the Royal Air Force, they play important roles in recruiting for the RAF and supporting UK industry overseas. But their remit extends further still. For the past 47 years the general public has come to regard the Red Arrows as a source of national pride and a symbol of what defines the 'Best of British'. The iconic Diamond Nine formation and red, white and blue smoke have become imprinted on the hearts of the nation and are an important part of our cultural heritage.

Whilst the job of impressing the public with their dynamic formation flying and precision aerobatics falls to those flying the nine red aircraft, the true unsung heroes of the Team are the support personnel, known as the Blues. Consisting of nearly 80 personnel and representing nearly all of the support branches and trades of the Royal Air Force, it is the dedication, commitment and professionalism of the Blues that ensures that the busy display season is possible. With many having recently served with distinction on operations in Afghanistan and Iraq, they work tirelessly to ensure that the standard of the Team being presented to the public is nothing short of exceptional.

This book provides a unique insight into life on the Red Arrows and tells the story of a close knit team of men and women whose job is to represent the Royal Air Force and act as ambassadors for their nation. Not only does it capture the essence of Éclat, it adds a personal touch in describing everyday life on the Team. Being a part of the Red Arrows is a childhood dream for many and the reality is every bit as rewarding. The stunning photography throughout this book captures the passion and dedication of a team intent on representing the very best of British and being the best aerobatic team in the world.

Éclat.

Squadron Leader Ben Murphy
Officer Commanding and Team Leader of the Royal Air Force
Aerobatic Team – the Red Arrows, 2010 and 2011

Acknowledgements

A project of this size requires the help and support of many people, who have contributed in different ways to make this book possible. The author would like to offer his sincere thanks to the following:

To all the team at RAFAT – working with you all under some difficult circumstances has been inspirational. Without your help and support throughout, the book would not have been possible. To the 2011 team members: Sqn Ldr Ben Murphy (Red 1); Flt Lt Chris Lyndon-Smith (Red 2); the late Flt Lt Sean Cunningham (Red 3); the late Flt Lt Jon Egging (Red 4); Flt Lt Kirsty Stewart (Red 5); Flt Lt David Montenegro (Red 6); Flt Lt Ben Plank (Red 7); Flt Lt Dave Davies (Red 8); Flt Lt Zane Sennett (Red 9); Sqn Ldr Graeme Bagnall (Red 10); Sqn Ldr Ross Priday (SEngO); Flt Lt Adam Littler (JEngO and Circus 1); WO Alan Murray BEM (Team Adjutant); Flt Sgt Steve Cox (Flt Sgt Engineering); SAC Geraldine Beaton (Circus 2); Cpl Dave Howard (Circus 3); Cpl Scott Aston (Circus 4); Cpl Kev Smith (Circus 5); Cpl Jamie Hatcher (Circus 6); SAC Simon Watkins (Circus 7); Sgt Matt Lord (Circus 8 and Circus Leader); SAC Joe Sproat (Circus 9) and Cpl Chris Moss (Circus 10).

To the new 2012 team members: Sqn Ldr Jim Turner (Red 1); Flt Lt Martin Pert (Red 2); Flt Lt Mike Child (Red 3); Flt Lt James McMillan (Red 4); Sqn Ldr Martin Higgins (Red 5); Sqn Ldr Mike Ling (Red 10); SAC Glenn Jones (Circus 2); SAC Nick Williams (Circus 3); Cpl Lyndon Picken (Circus 4); Cpl Jamie Hatcher (Circus 5); Cpl Lee Barnes (Circus 6); SAC James Frost (Circus 7); SAC Glynn West (Circus 8); Sgt Tim Elton (Circus 9 and Circus Leader); SAC Simon Watkins (Circus 10).

Special thanks go to Sqn Ldr Liz Parker (Team Manager), whose patience and tolerance I tested on so many occasions.

To the Photographic Section at RAF Scampton: Cpl Graham Taylor, SAC Dan Herrick and SAC Rob Travis, who allowed me access to their archive, assisted with research and pointed me in the right direction at Scampton on many occasions.

For providing access to the Hawk Replacement Programme at RAF Shawbury, I must thank John Dawson and Leigh Barnes of FB Helicopters. For providing access to the Great Ormond Street Hospital and assisting with clearing the photographs for publication, I would like to thank Lottie Wilkins.

For providing media facilities at airshows and events, and getting me close to the action, I would like to thank: Richard Arquati at RIAT; Keith Moughton at the Lowestoft Seafront Air Festival; Tony Shipp MBE at the Cromer Carnival; Emma Wilkinson at Airbourne Eastbourne.

For providing a wonderful selection of images to help with illustrating the book, I would like to thank: Mike Jorgenson of Action Air Images; Tim Kershaw, curator at the Russell Adams Collection; Peter R March; Ted Neville at Cody Images; Sarah Padley at QinetiQ/ETPS; Sqn Ldr Ross Priday; Dean Tasker, communications manager at BAe Systems; United States Navy; Oliver Wilson; and, finally, to Tom Clayton and David Hutton for providing the very special access to the BAe Heritage Group facilities.

I would like to send very special thanks to Dr Emma Egging, Nicky Cunningham and Flt Lt James Heath for providing assistance at such a very difficult time.

At Haynes Publishing, I would like to thank Jonathan Falconer, Sophie Blackman and Jane Hutchings for keeping me on track whenever I wavered.

A very special thank you goes to EJ van Koningsveld and his wife Jose. EJ opened up his wonderful collection of spectacular and creative images of the Red Arrows to me, and so many of these grace the pages of this book. If that were not enough, EJ and Jose insisted in having all their reproduction fees paid directly to the Jon Egging Trust. What more can be said?

Finally, sincere thanks to my wife Carol and sons Sam and Oliver. Thank you for your patience and support throughout the project. I couldn't have done it without you.

Bibliography

Ellis, Ken, *Wrecks & Relics*, 21st edn, Crecy Publishing, 2008

March, Peter R, *Hawk Comes of Age*, The Royal Air Force Benevolent Fund Enterprises, 1995

Mason, Francis K, *Hawker Aircraft Since 1920*, 3rd edn, Putnam Aeronautical Books, 1991

Thetford, Owen, *Aircraft of the Royal Air Force Since 1918*, 8th edn, Putnam Aeronautical Books, 1988

Watkins, David, *The History of RAF Aerobatic Teams From 1920*, Pen & Sword Aviation, 2010

Watson Smith, Ian, *RAF at Home, the History of RAF Air Displays From 1920*, Pen & Sword Aviation, 2010

Websites

www.ejection-history.org.uk (downloaded 16 May 2011)

www.sky-flash.com (downloaded 15 December 2011)

www.thunder-and-lightnings.co.uk (downloaded 6 July 2011)

Introduction

Nine aircraft, 60 engineers, 47 years flying and 4,410 displays performed in 54 different countries – these are some of the amazing statistics for the world's premier jet aerobatic formation display team.

Is there anyone in the UK who hasn't heard of the Red Arrows? Are there many people who haven't seen the Reds perform? Most people who watch them see nine pilots and their shiny red jets performing remarkable formation aerobatics. It is what they are meant to see. Why would they see anything else? Perhaps, it is similar to the swan syndrome – gliding elegantly above the water while paddling furiously below it!

Behind the scenes and away from the public gaze the team is a hive of activity. For the engineers there is a strategic juggle with limited airframes, limited Adour 151 engines and limited smoke-generating equipment. The airframes are ageing – some joined the team in 1977, most are 30 years old – but at least they are solid and reliable.

The cost of the team in 2011 was around £8.9 million pounds and £9.2 million is budgeted for 2012. While the numbers may, at first glance, appear relatively large, in real terms the benefits provided by the Red Arrows are extensive and they offer the public excellent value for money. They showcase the excellence of the Royal Air Force, provide an effective recruitment tool (just ask any of the current team what encouraged them to join the Royal Air Force) and act as ambassadors for Great Britain plc when appearing overseas. Many major aviation contracts have been 'influenced' by the presence of the Red Arrows in that particular country.

What is the future for the team? Well, funding has been approved through to 2015, at least.

During the research and writing of this book, I was offered unlimited access – both photographic and interviews: go anywhere (within safety margins), shoot anything, talk to anyone. 'We have nothing to hide,' was the policy at squadron level (although not always so, higher up the chain). Everyone offered their assistance willingly, and with enthusiasm and genuine interest.

What makes the Red Arrows so special? Yes, the Reds are superb pilots – the very best. After all, they have been handpicked to do the job.

Supporting the Reds are the Blues – slick, resourceful, efficient and professional – a credit to the Air Force and always helpful: offering me a quiet word, making sure I didn't get in the way, suggesting when something interesting may be happening or pointing me to the best spot for the picture.

Aside from the 'Boss', everyone in the Red Arrows has volunteered and faced a long and arduous selection process to win their place on the team. Together, they demonstrate the very highest level of teamwork.

For me, personally, the best memories were watching the Red Arrows in front of the public at the Royal International Air Tattoo and at Airbourne Eastbourne – not the spectacular formation flying which you simply take for granted, but the interface with the public that followed the flying. It was the continual answering of questions, signing of autographs, posing for pictures, chatting and maintaining the Red Arrows' smile. Their popularity among the public has to be seen to be believed – they are almost hero-worshipped. Each one the team has incredible patience and always has time for people. They politely answered even the daftest of questions and they found some time to play football with the children at Eastbourne. Most importantly, they *always* had a smile – and after a many hours in the cockpit, that was probably the toughest part of the day.

Then there were the occasions I spent on the ramp at Scampton, watching and photographing the Circus and other engineers going about their business in an organised, efficient and enthusiastic manner. They had very little time to refuel the aircraft, replenish the dye tanks (no smoke – no show), maintain and prepare the aircraft for the next Red Arrows' performance. For them – all volunteers and working outside in all weather – they have the very best job in the world.

I accompanied the Red Arrows to the Great Ormond Street Hospital for Children in December 2011, during their annual Christmas visit. The impact their presence had on the staff and the children's parents was enormous. Not one of the children appeared overawed by the presence of the Reds, and one or two of the cheekier children had team members running around for them! I watched members helping young children – some recovering from serious injuries or treatment – build and fly small paper Red Arrows aeroplanes. The Reds then received flying lessons from the children on just how they should fly them correctly. The visit was all quite humbling. When the time came to depart, there was no rush to leave the hospital, no request for an autograph or a photograph with one or more of the team was denied.

Being part of the Red Arrows is not so much a job, but a way of life. As a member of the Red Arrows you are either a Red or a Blue. Regardless of the colour of the overall you wear, you are always an important part of *The Team*.

Ladies and gentlemen, I give you the Red Arrows.

Keith Wilson
Ramsey, Cambridgeshire
February 2012

History of the
Red Arrows

The first organised international air meet was the Semaine d'Aviation de la Champagne (The Champagne Region's Great Aviation Week), held at a racetrack on the Bethany Plain outside Reims, France, between 22 and 29 August 1909. Around a quarter of a million people attended and they were entertained by the likes of Louis Blériot, Henri Farman, Alberto Santos-Dumont and Glenn Curtiss. The week's programme included various trials and races and culminated with the running of the Gordon Bennett Cup, with a first prize of £1,500. Some great pioneering aircraft were present, including the Farman biplane, the Wright Flyer and the Antoinette monoplane.

Interestingly, the Reims meeting also witnessed the first public demonstration of aerobatics by self-taught aviator Eugène Lefébvre, in a Wright Flyer. Many considered his 'stunts' to be outstandingly daring while others remained cautious. It was a widely held belief by aviators at the time that to venture from straight and level flight – apart from gentle banks and turns – was to invite disaster. As if to emphasise this point, Lefébvre was killed in a flying accident the following month.

First military air display

The RAF Hendon Aerial Pageant, on 3 July 1920, was the first military air display ever held. It was the creation of Lord Trenchard, the first Marshal of the Royal Air Force and Chief of the Air Staff, who was also the controller of the then RAF Memorial Fund. He felt that an air display would be an imaginative way of raising funds while also providing a good public relations exercise for the Royal Air Force. Although the event was poorly advertised it attracted a crowd estimated at 40,000. It was run with typical military precision. The programme was dominated by wartime aircraft, including the Bristol Fighter, Sopwith Camel and SE5a, while most of the aerobatic demonstrations were provided by veterans of the First World War. It also featured one of the first aerial display teams – five Sopwith Snipes from the Central Flying School (CFS) at Wittering – which brought the crowd to its feet with a display of simultaneous looping and Immelmann turns. The show was considered an overwhelming success and raised £7,261 for the Memorial Fund.

With this success behind them, the Air Staff decided that the pageant would become a regular event and perhaps, more importantly, form an important part of the RAF training programme. Between 1920 and 1937, squadrons vied with one another to appear at this prestigious show, which was seen as the culmination of their training and an opportunity to demonstrate their flying skills to the public. By 1929, as a result of the 'crazy flying' routines of standard training aircraft of the Flying Training Schools and the highly disciplined formation flying of the various squadrons' aerobatic flights, Hendon had become one of the great events of the London season alongside the Royal Tournament at Olympia and the Aldershot Military Tattoo.

Coloured smoke

Innovative routines had always been used by display teams to entertain the crowds, but the first to use trailing coloured smoke to enhance an aerobatic display was demonstrated by a pair of Gloster Grebes from the Aeroplane and Armament Experimental Establishment (A&AEE) at Martlesham Heath, Suffolk, in 1929. With a succession of aircraft supplied by the A&AEE at the annual Hendon Pageant, the RAF waited another five years until 19(F) Squadron from Duxford fitted 'smoke-making' apparatus to its Bristol Bulldogs for its appearance at the 1934 pageant, using smoke in the RAF colours of red, white and blue.

Another innovation was tied-together aerobatics, which was pioneered at the 1930 event by the Siskins of 43(F) Squadron. Three flights of three aircraft performed with their wingtips attached by lengths of rubber cord, flying a series of loops and flights in line abreast before completing their display with a Prince of Wales Feathers at the top of a loop, thereby breaking the cords.

The final RAF display was held in 1937 and was possibly the largest and most successful of the 18 annual displays – with more than 600 aircraft taking part and 195,000 people attending the event. In 1938, the Air Council announced that it was discontinuing the RAF displays

➤ At the RAF
Display at Hendon in
June 1937, five Gloster
Gauntlets of No 66
Squadron, led by Flt Lt
Vintras, displayed,
using green, orange
and white smoke to
good effect against
the grey clouds.
(Cody Images/1016963)

as Hendon was considered 'too small for modern fast aeroplanes'. The intimacy of the Empire Air Days, where the public could inspect aeroplanes and equipment at close quarters was to become a far greater success.

Empire Air Days

The Empire Air Days began in 1934 when the Air League of the British Empire promoted a scheme to create a greater interest in aviation among the general public. Not only were active RAF stations opened to the public, but activities at civil aerodromes, flying clubs and aircraft factories were revealed to a much wider audience. In 1934, 41 RAF stations, 40 flying clubs and various aeroplane firms opened to the public; and these were attended by an audience estimated at 100,000 people. By 1938, the numbers of stations participating had increased considerably, as had the numbers attending – estimated at 420,000, despite poor weather. In 1939, when the last Empire Air Day was held on 20 May, 63 RAF stations and 16 civil aerodromes opened their gates and attendances reached nearly 850,000. The largest number was at Northolt where 56,000 attended.

After the Second World War it was decided to absorb the pre-war Empire Air Days and the Battle of Britain commemorations into one Royal Air Force Day. On 15 September 1945, the first post-war Battle of Britain Display Day was held when 93 RAF Stations opened their doors to the public.

▼ Three Meteor T7s of the Central Flying School's (CFS) Meteorites display team emulate a similar formation flown by a pre-war CFS Avro Tutor team in 1933. Sqn Ldr George Brabyn flies his Meteor T7, WF852, inverted, with wingmen Flt Lts James and Price (WH241/N-D and WA691/Y-D) in tight formation during a photographic sortie from Little Rissington on 28 March 1952 for the school's 1952 Christmas card. *(Peter R March)*

Jet formation aerobatics

In July 1947, 54 Squadron at Odiham laid claim to being the world's first jet formation aerobatic team when it took three Vampires to the *Grande International Aeronautical Gala* at Evere, Belgium. In the following year, the team was temporarily absorbed into the Aerobatic Squadron, which was established from all the RAF Odiham Vampire display teams especially for a goodwill tour of the USA and Canada. In July 1948, six Vampires went into the record books as the first jet fighters to cross the Atlantic from east to west, before successfully taking part in exercises with the USAF and displaying at airshows in Canada and the USA.

In the early post-war years, with more than 63 fighter squadrons in the RAF, almost every squadron had a formation aerobatic team and one or two designated display pilots. While flying discipline for operational flying was vital and of a very high standard, the same disciplines were not always found in display flying and accidents were numerous.

The CFS was re-formed at RAF Little Rissington, Gloucestershire, in May 1946. Initial equipment consisted of Tiger Moths and Harvards, but by May 1952, the CFS (Basic) Squadron operated at RAF South Cerney with Harvard, Prentice and Provost trainers, while the CFS (Advanced) Squadron at Little Rissington had Provosts, Meteors and Vampires. During early post-war years there was no official CFS aerobatic team but the delivery of the first Meteor jet trainers in April 1949 aroused great excitement among the instructors at Little Rissington. The initial idea was a four-ship team that would perform a series of tied-together formations – but the idea was quietly dropped. The CFS did contribute 37 Harvards to a mass fly-past at Farnborough in 1950, in a tribute to the Queen. In 1952, the next

Meteor formation team was formed especially for the creation of the school's 1952 Christmas card, and to re-enact a formation that had previously been flown by four Avro Tutors back in 1933.

Later in that year, Flt Lt Caryl Gordon was ordered to assemble and lead the first official post-war CFS Meteor display team. It was among the earliest RAF aerobatic teams to be given a name – the Meteorites – consisting of four Meteor T7 aircraft. In 1954 the team was renamed the Pelicans Meteor Display Team – the name inspired by the crest of the CFS. By 1957, the Meteor Team had been disbanded so the mantle of 'Official' CFS Aerobatic Display Team was transferred to a team of four Provost T1s, which became known as the Sparrows.

When the Jet Provost T1 arrived at Little Rissington in November 1957, the CFS was asked to form a team of four aircraft to appear at the 1958 SBAC Display at Farnborough. The Jet Provost T1 was not ideal for display flying – being seriously underpowered – so the display routine was somewhat limited. Adopting the rather uninspiring title of the CFS Jet Aerobatic Team, the aircraft were painted in a special red-and-white colour scheme and flew 17 displays during the 1958 season.

The second CFS Display Team was formed in January 1960 with four Jet Provost T3s and performed at 30 official displays in its first year. It continued to perform the following year, then in March 1962 the new season's team was formed and the number of aircraft was increased to five – utilising the newly delivered T4 variant of the Jet Provost. Renamed the Red Pelicans, it completed 29 shows. In 1963, the Red Pelicans was nominated as the 'Official' RAF aerobatic team and a sixth aircraft was added; they were all painted in a new all-over, Day-Glo red colour scheme.

A tight formation of four Meteor T7s (WH241, WG962, WA615 and WA688) of the CFS's Meteorites aerobatic team looping over Oxfordshire on 24 July 1953. *(Jet Age Museum/Russell Adams)*

Four Meteor F8s, including WH480 and WA994, from No 41 Squadron at Biggin Hill, c1953. *(Peter R March)*

Hawker Hunter arrives

Meanwhile, CFS was not getting things all its own way on the air display scene as a number of Fighter Command squadrons had excellent display teams entertaining airshow visitors. In 1954, the year after the Hawker Hunter entered service, the first Fighter Command display team – the Black Nights – was formed by No 54 Squadron. The Hawker Hunter is widely regarded as the best mount ever chosen for the RAF's aerobatic teams. Various squadron teams were formed: from 1957 to 1962 it was the turn of No 111 Squadron's Black Arrows and from 1961 it was 92 Squadron's Blue Diamonds.

When Sqn Ldr Roger Topp took command of No 111 Squadron in January 1955, they were still operating Meteors, but were in the process of re-equipping the squadron with Hunter F4s, which began

⋀ Designed to impress: eight Hunter F6s of Treble One Squadron – the Black Arrows – in tight formation. In 1956, No 111 Squadron Hunter display team had been nominated as the official aerobatic team of No 11 Group – initially equipped with four Hunter F4s, before being replaced with Hunter F6s in November 1956. All the squadron's aircraft were painted in their trademark all-over gloss-black colour scheme from March 1957. *(Cody Images/1016982)*

≪ Four Hunters F1s of No 54 Squadron, the Black Knights, practising for the SBAC show at Farnborough on 5 September 1955. No 54 Squadron achieved a number of notable firsts with its Meteor and Hunter jets: first post-war, jet formation display team; first jet display team to cross the Atlantic; first RAF jet aerobatic team to perform in Canada and the USA; first RAF jet formation team to incorporate smoke into its display routine; first official RAF Fighter Command Hunter display team; and first Hunter formation display team to appear at the SBAC Show, Farnborough. *(Cody Images/1016981)*

Hunter F6s in the Big Nine, up from North Weald in 1957. Between March and September 1957, the Black Arrows of Treble One Squadron performed 24 shows in the UK, France, Italy and Norway, as well as a week at the SBAC Show, Farnborough in September. *(Cody Images/1016972)*

➤ No 74 Squadron began conversion from Meteor F8 to Hunter F4 aircraft in February 1957, until being re-equipped with the F6 in November of the same year. When the squadron moved to Coltishall in June 1959, a four-ship display team – known locally as the Vicar's Garden Party – was formed and flew a few displays that year. Tragically, pilot Pete Budd was killed in a night-flying accident two days after a show at RAF Leuchars and the team was disbanded. *(Peter R March)*

A never-to-be-repeated spectacle of a formation loop by 22 Hunters, seen here on 28 August 1958 during a rehearsal for the SBAC Show at Farnborough. Led by Squadron Leader Roger Topp and the Black Arrows of Treble One Squadron, the spectacle was achieved by utilising additional Command Reserve aircraft and 'borrowing' pilots from other squadrons. After performing at Farnborough, the mass formation was repeated twice at Wattisham the following week – the second time for the AOC-in-C, Air Chief Marshal Sir Thomas Pike, who sanctioned the original routine. *(Cody Images/1016977)*

experimental schemes were suggested and it was eventually decided to paint the Hunters in an overall gloss-black scheme. The formation would increase to nine aircraft and a 40gal diesel tank was installed in the ammunition bay of each aircraft, to provide a more effective method of producing smoke. It was also in this year that the team was unofficially named the Black Arrows by Roger Topp.

Topp Twenty for Farnborough

In order to make the squadron's appearance at the 1958 Farnborough Show 'a more spectacular and memorable event', Topp suggested to the then Air Officer Commanding-in-Chief, Fighter Command, Air Chief Marshal Sir Thomas Pike, that a mass formation loop would be an ideal way to close the show.

Originally, Topp wanted to fly 20 aircraft at the Farnborough Show (which rather inevitably, was to be called the Topp Twenty), but the formation was considered too long for the aircraft to stay in position over the top of the loop – especially for those aircraft on the outside of the formation. The solution was simple: increase the frontage to seven aircraft with three in line astern; this made for a wider but shorter formation

in June of that year. Once the squadron's conversion to the Hunter was complete, Roger Topp was quick to exploit the performance of the aircraft and by March 1956 his four-ship team had been formed. The following month they were nominated as the official aerobatic team of No 11 Group and with their public appearance at Bordeaux on 13 May 1956 they stole the show. Permission to use a fifth aircraft was granted in August and was first shown to the public during the Battle of Britain displays in September.

The following year, Treble One was selected as Fighter Command's leading aerobatic team – now equipped with the Hunter F6, which had begun joining the squadron in January 1957. The squadron was also allowed to paint the aircraft in a special colour scheme. Various

The successors to the Black Arrows were the Blue Diamonds of 92 Squadron, also equipped with the Hunter F6. The team flew a variety of formation formats from 9 to as many as 16 aircraft, then increased to 18 in 1962. They were the principal Fighter Command display team in 1961 and 1962 and were photographed with 16 aircraft while practising close to their home base at RAF Leconfield in June 1961. *(Peter R March)*

The Blue Diamonds of 92 Squadron were photographed during a press facility on the ramp of their home base at Leconfield in June 1961. *(Peter R March)*

which, although quite difficult to fly, was just a little easier to loop. That made 21 aircraft, but an extra aircraft could be accommodated in the centre line so 22 aircraft it was. This incredible feat was achieved by using additional aircraft and pilots from other squadrons, all of them volunteers. The first 22-aircraft formation was flown on 22 August and established a new world record. The mass formation loop by Treble One Squadron was then performed at Farnborough. Will anyone who witnessed the spectacular event ever forget what they saw that day?

In November 1959, No 92 Squadron was nominated as the official RAF reserve aerobatic team. The squadron had provided a five-ship Hunter F6 formation team in 1958 but was now allowed to increase the number of aircraft to six. In 1961, the squadron was nominated as the RAF's official aerobatic team and set about providing a routine to rival that of Treble One's. The team featured nine aircraft, which were all painted in a new and distinctive royal blue colour scheme. For their appearance at Wildenrath, Germany, on 22 April 1961, they were billed as the Falcons, but a German newspaper coined the name Blaue Diamanten (Blue Diamonds) and the name was officially approved. In July 1961, the Blue Diamonds flew the Diamond Sixteen formation for the first time – featuring 16 Hunters – in preparation for the forthcoming Society of British Aircraft Companies (SBAC) show. After their appearance at Farnborough, the Diamond Sixteen formation was successfully repeated by the team at a number of displays across the UK. Sadly, 92 Squadron's time as the RAF's official aerobatic display team was short-lived when an EE Lightning squadron was chosen for 1962.

⋀ **Such was the demand for the principal teams on Battle of Britain Day, and to accommodate as many of the open stations as possible, the Blue Diamonds of 92 Squadron would give a display with their full complement at one or two locations before splitting into two still substantial aerobatic formations to display at other stations.** *(Peter R March)*

⋁ **Four Jet Provost T1s of the CFS's Jet Aerobatic Team in 1958. The team flew 17 displays during the season, including the SBAC show at Farnborough in September.** *(Alex Wickham via Peter R March)*

➤ **By 1960, the CFS had formed an aerobatic display team of Jet Provost T3s. The formation – consisting of XM411/R-G, XM413/R-H, XM425/R-L and XM428/R-M – was photographed over the CFS home of Little Rissington airfield (seen just below formation) on 6 July 1960.** *(Jet Age Museum/Russell Adams)*

Lightnings make their mark

In June 1960, 74 Squadron became the first operational unit to be equipped with the Lightning F1. It possessed an initial rate of climb in excess of 50,000ft/min and could reach its operational ceiling in less than two minutes. With its Mach 2 capability in level flight, it could more than double the Hunter's speed. No 74 Squadron's initial conversion from Hunter to Lightning was hampered by a slow rate of delivery, poor serviceability and a shortage of spares. By the end of August it had only seven Lightnings on strength, so when HQ Fighter Command ordered the squadron to display a four-ship team at Farnborough in September the squadron was really up against it. But operating from Boscombe Down and utilising seven aircraft, make it they did.

By February 1961, the squadron had its full complement of 12 aircraft on strength and were able to rehearse with larger formations for the forthcoming Paris Air Show in June, as well as Farnborough in September. For their daily appearances at the 1961 Farnborough show, the Tigers of 74 Squadron took 12 aircraft into the air – the Diamond Nine plus three air spares – but had to borrow aircraft from other units to make this happen. On 24 April 1962, 74 Squadron was notified that it had been chosen as the RAF Fighter Command aerobatic team, which brought further disruptions to training and operational commitments.

Although the squadron Lightnings had been previously restricted to the black-and-yellow triangular markings on the nose of the aircraft and the unit's tiger head on a white disc on the fins, for the 1962 Farnborough show appearance the aircraft were repainted with gloss-black fins and rudders and fuselage spines; the tiger's head was retained on the fin.

In June 1960, No 74 Squadron at RAF Coltishall became the first operational unit to be equipped with the mach 2 English Electric Lightning F1. Nearest the camera is XM143/A belonging to then team leader of the Tigers formation display team, Sqn Ldr John Howe. *(Cody Images/ 1016962)*

The Air Ministry had decided that as a gap-filler between formation passes at Farnborough, and while 74 Squadron was repositioning, a formation of 92 Squadron Hunters would perform in the interludes. The work-up commenced in July and the first 74/92 squadron formation was flown on 24 August. After joint displays for the C-in-C and media, they deployed to Farnborough. Despite all the work involved, the combined formation display of 16 Hunters from 92 Squadron and 7 Lightnings from 74 Squadron was only made on one occasion at Farnborough – 9 September.

The Tigers of 74 Squadron had become the first aerobatic display team to fly Mach 2 aircraft and brought a new dimension to airshow crowds with its reheat take-offs and near-vertical climbs; a routine which undoubtedly stirred the imagination of many and set the standards for successive teams to emulate.

No 56 Squadron re-equipped with Lightning F1As in January 1961. In October 1962, the squadron was unofficially notified that it had been nominated to represent the RAF at the Paris Air Show in June 1963. The team soon became know as the Firebirds and squadron aircraft were repainted in a distinctive new colour scheme comprising deep scarlet leading edges to the wings and tailplane, and to the spine and fin. A large white disc featuring the unit's traditional 'Phoenix' emblem was added to the fin.

To produce enough smoke for the display routine, modifications were made to the port flap tank to hold 33gal of diesel and the interior

Five Lightning F1s of No 74 Squadron. For their appearance at the SBAC Show, Farnborough in 1962, the aircraft were repainted with a gloss-black fin, rudder and fuselage spine and the squadron's tiger head motif was retained on the fin. With the mach 2 EE Lightnings, the Tigers brought a new dimension to airshow crowds. Sadly, XM142/B (nearest the camera) was written off on 24 April 1963. *(Cody Images/1016963)*

plumbing was reworked to incorporate a small nozzle protruding above the bottom reheat pipe between the two engines. By wiring a small electric pump to the gun circuit, diesel fuel was injected into the jet efflux when the gun switch was selected. For the display season, most of the squadron Lightnings had their AI23 radar units locked in the neutral position, while others had the units replaced with lead ballast.

Diamond Nine manoeuvre

The main feature of the team's display routine was the Diamond Nine formation roll, which had been pioneered by 74 Squadron in 1961. To achieve the manoeuvre, the team combined two separate sections: the front five aircraft (Red section) and the box of four aircraft (Green section). All display practices were carried out with the pilots gradually working up in pairs, then in threes and finally five, until they were considered sufficiently proficient to fly as a complete formation of nine. The team was expensive to operate, and because it also had to maintain operational status, it performed only a limited number of displays – mainly towards the end of the season. The actual display routine started with a reheat, stream take-off with ten aircraft rotating at three-second intervals – the tenth aircraft being the spare whose pilot checked the cloud base.

With the conclusion of the display season the authorities decided that the Lightning 'was a highly sophisticated supersonic fighter

Nine Lightning F1s of No 56 Squadron – the Firebirds – displaying their Diamond Nine formation roll at Farnborough in September 1963. Serial numbers include XM164, 163, 137, 146, 144, 165, 143, 138 and 140. *(Peter R March)*

aircraft unsuitable for the type of aerobatic flying that an airshow demanded'. The Lightning also 'lacked the impact of the previous Hunter teams on a display crowd' and 'proved too expensive to divert from its front-line duties'. In October 1963, a milestone decision was taken to discontinue any further Lightning premier display teams and the future commitment for providing the RAF Aerobatic Team would be passed to RAF Flying Training Command.

Gnat trials

Designed as a two-seat advanced trainer development of the Folland Gnat fighter to replace the Vampire T11, the Gnat T1 was delivered to the CFS at Little Rissington in February 1962. However, earlier flight trials at the A&AEE at Boscombe Down had indicated some concern with the Gnat's pitch sensitivity and subsequently recommended a complete ban on formation aerobatics.

In November 1962, Lee Jones, an experienced formation display pilot who had led the Black Arrows, was posted to CFS and was one of the first to undergo the Gnat conversion course before being sent to No 4 FTS at RAF Valley on Anglesey. He quickly recognised the Gnat's potential as a formation aerobatic platform and persistently campaigned for a station display team and, despite previous misgivings, was eventually granted his wish. Following an internal selection process among the instructors at

⋀ **A Lightning T5 (XM989/X) and nine Lightning F1As of No 56 Squadron – the Firebirds – on the ramp at Wattisham during a press facility on 10 May 1963. Eleven official airshows were performed by the squadron in 1963, but at the end of the year it was decided that the Lightning was a 'highly sophisticated supersonic fighter aircraft unsuitable for the type of aerobatic flying that an airshow demanded'. Consequently, the future commitment to provide the official RAF Aerobatic Team was passed to RAF Flying Training Command.** *(Peter R March)*

⋁ **In 1962, the CFS provided a five-ship display team of Jet Provost T4s – known as the Red Pelicans. Here, four of its aircraft, including XP553/44 and XP573/49, are seen performing at the SBAC Show at Farnborough in September of that year.** *(Cody Images/1016968)*

➤ **In the following year, the CFS Red Pelicans were nominated as the official RAF aerobatic team. A sixth aircraft was added to the formation and all the aircraft were repainted in a new all-over Day-Glo red colour scheme.** *(Peter R March)*

Formed in 1965 at RAF Manby as the RAF College of Air Warfare Formation Aerobatic Team, it was renamed the Macaws in March 1968. The pilots were all Qualified Flying Instructors (QFIs) of the School of Refresher Flying at Manby. The team made its public debut at Elstree on 5 June 1965 and its final appearance at Luxeuil, France, in September 1973, falling victim to the 1974 oil crisis. This July 1972 photograph features Jet Provost T4s XP558, XR701, XP672 and XS219. *(Peter R March)*

Having been formed in 1969 by No 1 Flying Training Squadron (FTS) at RAF Linton-on-Ouse, the Linton Blades continued to display through to the end of the 1973 season. Here, four of their aircraft (XA296/57, XW305/63, XW304/62 and XW308/67) pass over the iconic Fylingdales site in 1971. *(Peter R March)*

Valley, the five-ship team was selected – five aircraft offering more variety of formation patterns than existing four-ship teams.

Early formation practice started in February 1964 – but did not begin in earnest before July – and all training had to fit in with existing busy training schedules. Although envisaged as a team of five aircraft, initial doubts over maintaining serviceability of the Gnat found the team being allocated nine airframes. To ensure the RAF Valley team did not conflict with the official RAF team from Little Rissington – the Red Pelicans – it was decided to paint the Gnats in the traditional Flying Training Command high-visibility yellow colour scheme. The aircraft were resprayed at Dunsfold and the first three aircraft collected from there on 5 June.

Call sign 'Yellowjack'

The team had adopted the radio call sign 'Yellowjack' to distinguish itself from student formations at the school. A local reporter – who was watching a display from the control tower – heard the radio call 'Yellowjack running in' and in his subsequent article referred to the

team as the Yellowjacks. The name stuck and has since passed into aviation history.

The team gave its first public display at RNAS Culdrose on 25 June 1964 and then followed this with a display at RAF Brawdy – both to rave reviews. They were asked to appear at Farnborough in September, alongside the RAF's official team – the Red Pelicans. It was to be a challenging show as Farnborough audiences had become used to mass formations and big squadron Hunter and Lightning displays. Someone suggested that the two teams should appear alongside each other – to increase the impact of both – so the Jet Provosts were deployed to Valley for three weeks in early August to work-up a suitable joint routine.

The Farnborough show was hailed a great success, especially for the Yellowjacks. Two weeks later, the team gave the last public displays at Biggin Hill and Gaydon; it was disbanded in October. Despite its short existence, the Yellowjacks had a major impact on subsequent RAF aerobatic display teams, especially the later formation of the Gnat-equipped Red Arrows.

∀ **Five Gnat T1s of the formation aerobatic team of No 4 FTS, RAF Valley –unofficially known as the Yellowjacks – performing at the SBAC Show Farnborough in September 1964 in their striking high-visibility yellow colour scheme.** *(Peter R March)*

∆ ➢ **Two views of the RAF Gnat Aerobatic Team – the Yellowjacks – from No 4 Flying Training School, RAF Valley, in July 1964. To ensure the RAF Valley team did not conflict with the official RAF team from Little Rissington – the Red Pelicans – it was decided to paint the Gnats in the traditional Flying Training Command high-visibility yellow colour scheme. There had been suggestions during the work-up that the new colour scheme made the aircraft difficult to identify in less-than-favourable weather conditions and for a brief period during July, one of the Gnats (XR992) had its fin painted black. The experiment proved inconclusive and was dropped after a few practice sorties.** *(Jet Age Museum/Russell Adams)*

Formation of a permanent RAF display team

With the increasing sophistication and cost of fighter aircraft, as well as the considerable disruption to their units, the RAF decided to form the first permanent display team – known as the Royal Air Force Aerobatic Team (RAFAT) – administered by the CFS at Little Rissington. The advantages of a permanent team were seen at the time as numerous: to raise the British and RAF prestige, as well as flying standards and morale within the services; to stimulate recruiting; and to publicise the merits of British aviation in the world market place. Looking back over the years, this final aspect has been carried out to considerable effect.

The first choice to be made for the team was which aircraft to fly and a variety were considered by a working party set up in early 1965. They included the Jet Provost (considered a retrograde step), Hawker Hunter (considered obsolete), Lightning (too expensive and would use up valuable fatigue life on the airframes), Hawker P1127 Kestrel (an attractive proposition), Sepecat Jaguar (considered suitable when *eventually* delivered to squadron service) and, of course, the Folland Gnat, although not without having a significant impact on RAF training.

The working party suggested the Hawker P1127, but this would not be available until 1970. Consequently, with few options and a good track record with the Yellowjacks, the Ministry of Defence (MoD) opted for the Folland Gnat – the type considered to be sleek, fast and highly manoeuvrable. The official name chosen was Red Arrows – 'Red' to retain the link with the CFS display team (Red Pelicans*),* while 'Arrows' would revive memories of the famous Black Arrows.

An MoD study concluded that ten airframes would be required to maintain the long-term success of the team. With the disbandment of the Yellowjacks in October 1964, all the airframes had been flown to RAF Kemble for overhaul. The opportunity was taken to respray them in an overall Post Office red colour scheme in keeping with the team's new identity. The first aircraft (XR540) was delivered on 1 February 1965 and the final aircraft (XS111) on 14 May.

The Red Arrows take off

The Red Arrows were formally constituted at RAF Fairford on 1 March 1965 and Lee Jones became the natural choice to lead the new team. While based at Little Rissington, the team used nearby Fairford for practice – the availability of a clear airfield was essential when working up. On 6 May the team gave its first display to the gathered media at Little Rissington and three days later, gave its first public display at the French National Air Meeting at Clermont-Ferrand. The team's first UK public display was at Biggin Hill on 15 May where the seven-Gnat team provided a 15-minute show in front of a crowd approaching 40,000. The team went on to complete 50 shows at 40 different venues during its first season. It was, clearly, just the start of much bigger things to come.

In February 1966, Ray Hanna was appointed team leader and, for the new season, it was decided to increase the number of pilots to nine. Despite the new establishment of nine pilots and ten aircraft, the MoD insisted that only seven-aircraft formations be flown as the team 'could not sustain a nine-ship formation with only one spare aircraft available'. However, the first nine-ship practice was flown on 18 March and a few months later the nine-

◁ On 23 April 1965, while based at RAF Fairford, the Red Arrows flew an air-to-air sortie with photographer Russell Adams. RAF Fairford is visible in the bottom left of this striking seven-ship view. Cameraship for the occasion was an Armstrong Whitworth Meteor NF14 flown by Flt Lt Tony Chaplin. *(Jet Age Museum/Russell Adams)*

▽ The 1966 Red Arrows team in classic Diamond Nine formation. *(Crown Copyright)*

△ In February 1966, Ray Hanna was appointed as team leader and the number of pilots in the team was increased from seven to nine. In this picture with Sqn Ldr Ray Hanna at the forefront are Flt Lt Derek Bell (Red 2), Flt Lt Bill Langworthy (Red 3), Flt Lt Peter Evans (Red 4), Flt Lt Roy Booth (Red 5), Flt Lt Henry Prince (Red 6), Flt Lt Timothy Nelson (red 7), Flt Lt Frank Hoare (Red 8) and Flt Lt Douglas McGregor (Red 9). *(Peter R March)*

◄ Early nine-ship image of the Red Arrows performing in the original all-over Post Office red colour scheme, c1966. (Peter R March)

➤ Six Gnat T1s of the Red Arrows practising at Kemble in 1971 ahead of a planned performance in front of HRH the Queen Mother. (Crown Copyright)

∨ During the winter of 1967, due to both a shortage of Gnat airframes as well as financial restraints imposed by the Treasury, the team was reduced to seven aircraft. Around the same time, the Gnats were repainted with full-chord red, white and blue tail fins as a first sign of the relaxation of the MoD ban on colourful paint schemes. In this view at Kemble in 1967, six aircraft feature the new colour scheme while the aircraft nearest the camera sports the original all-over Post Office red colour. (Peter R March)

ship formation was approved – in time to be flown in front of HRH The Duke of Edinburgh at Little Rissington on 8 July. The team moved to self-contained facilities at Kemble in September, but continued to practise at Fairford.

With 85 displays throughout Europe, 1966 proved a record-breaking year for the team. However, a study by the MoD concluded that there would not be enough aircraft to sustain the team in 1967 and 1968. There was some consideration of a Chivenor-based Hunter team or the CFS Red Pelicans to replace them, but in the end the Red Arrows won the day – with a reduced display complement of seven aircraft in 1967.

Having been repainted with a red, white and blue tail fin during winter maintenance, the start of the 1967 season was delayed by a routine grounding of all Gnat aircraft due to structural weaknesses. Despite this setback, the team went on to fly 77 displays.

The year 1968 marked the 50th Anniversary of the RAF, the climax of the Golden Jubilee Celebrations being the Royal Review at Abingdon. The team gave more than 100 displays in 12 months.

Good times, bad times

The following year it was decided to establish the Red Arrows on a permanent basis, as the equivalent of a standard RAF squadron, and increase the strength to 60 airmen. The team suffered its first fatal accident in 1969 when XR573 crashed at Kemble during routine formation practice, with the loss of Jerry Bowler.

During the work-up for 1970, two more aircraft were lost in an extraordinary accident on 16 December when Flt Lt Jack Rust's aircraft caught fire following an engine failure. He subsequently ejected 1 mile (1.6km) south of the airfield. Unfortunately, after being mistakenly told that it was his aircraft on fire, Flt Lt Dickie Duckett also ejected after being instructed to do so by his leader. Both aircraft came down in open countryside. Despite this setback, the team's winter work-up went well and the nine-ship team completed 89 displays.

Sadly, losses continued for the team. On 13 November 1970, the new team leader – Dennis Hazell – was seriously injured and prevented from participating in the 1971 season following an ejection incident after yet another engine failure during formation

practice. Training Command decided to investigate the cause of the significant numbers of engine failure incidents and suggested that on training sorties, other team members not involved in the sortie could sit in the back seat and record throttle movements. Unfortunately, when the Synchro Pair were practising their routine over Kemble on 20 January 1971, Red 6 (Euan Perreaux) and Red 7 (John Haddock) – accompanied by back-seaters Colin Armstrong and John Lewis, respectively – collided and both aircraft crashed onto the airfield. All four pilots were lost.

The incident made national news and questions were asked in Parliament. A plan was devised to continue the team, but with only seven aircraft; by the end of the year 73 displays had been completed.

The team was able to return to a nine-ship in 1972 and was asked to undertake a tour of Canada and the United States. Codenamed 'Operation Longbow', the full team, led by Sqn Ldr Ian Dick and accompanied by a pair of Hercules support aircraft, departed on the first leg of a five-week tour on 15 May. The team's first big display was at the Transpo 72 exhibition, Dulles, Washington – to an audience

estimated at 1.5 million. After a successful tour, the team returned to Kemble on 16 June.

The oil crisis in 1974 made things very difficult for the team. The restriction on flying hours meant a late start to the season in which only 59 displays were made. Continued restrictions in 1975 lead to only 76 displays, but did include trips to Norway, Denmark and Germany.

The year 1977 was one for landmarks. Restrictions were relaxed and the season was dominated by the Queen's Silver Jubilee celebrations. Two new manoeuvres were introduced into the display routine – 'Piccadilly' and the 'Jubilee Break' – specially devised in honour of the Queen. Among 109 displays flown in the year, the team was part of the mass flypast over Buckingham Palace on 11 June to celebrate the Queen's birthday. It achieved its 1,000th display at the Royal International Air Tattoo (RIAT) at Greenham Common on 26 June.

The team suffered another incident during a low-level manoeuvre on 3 March 1978 when the aircraft (XR981) crashed, killing both Flt Lt Steve Noble and his passenger, former team leader Wg Cdr Dennis Hazell. Despite this setback, the team completed 123 displays in the season.

⋀ Another striking view of the Diamond Nine formation captured going over the top of a loop. This image was most likely taken from a tail-mounted camera on the aircraft positioned just ahead of the formation. *(Crown Copyright)*

➤ In 1973 the Red Arrows' nine Folland Gnat T1s flew in formation with the British pre-production Concorde 01 (G-AXDN). At the time, the Concorde flight test programme was based at RAF Fairford while the Red Arrows were based close-by at RAF Kemble. *(Arthur Gibson/BAC pictures via RAF Scampton)*

A seven-ship Gnat formation of the Red Arrows showing the red, white and blue smoke system to good effect at the SBAC Show, Farnborough, on 11 September 1976.
(Keith Wilson)

Another view of the Red Arrows at Farnborough on 11 September 1976, this time with a nine-ship. It was to be the final year that the Red Arrows were to appear at the SBAC Show at Farnborough with Gnat T1 aircraft.
(Keith Wilson)

Λ **Nine Red Arrows' Gnats in Diamond Nine at the 1976 Farnborough Airshow.** *(Crown Copyright)*

Gnats give way to Hawks

In 1979, the team made its last public displays with the Gnat T1 at the Battle of Britain shows at Abingdon and St Athan on 15 September, followed by a private display at Valley. After 14 years of service with the Red Arrows, the Gnat was replaced by the new Hawk T1, the first aircraft (XX251) being delivered on 16 August. By the time the aircraft were withdrawn from use and allocated ground duties, the Gnats had completed a total of 1,292 displays and visited 18 countries.

Further deliveries of new Hawk aircraft were made towards the end of 1979 and by 29 October, nine aircraft had been delivered. Shortly afterwards, XX260 was damaged when the pilot experienced a loud rumbling sensation which he interpreted as engine surge and he departed the nine-ship formation. The aircraft ended up at the western end of Kemble's runway but was quickly repaired and returned to service in time for the official hand-over of the last aircraft at RAF Bitteswell on 15 November 1979.

To create the appropriate coloured smoke for its displays, a 70gal centreline smoke generating pod containing separate tanks for the diesel, as well as red and blue coloured dyes, was designed and fitted. The liquids are pumped into three separate outlet pipes, located on the rear fuselage, just above the engine jet pipe, permitting sufficient 'smoke' to allow five minutes of white and one minute of both red and blue. The team's Rolls Royce/Turbomeca Adour engines incorporate modifications to the fuel accelerator to provide a more rapid throttle response than that fitted to the standard Hawk.

In 1979, the team had ten aircraft available for the very first time for winter training. Consequently, the first nine-ship display practice was flown on 13 November and the first full display sequence on 20 December. Another first for the team was a winter training programme at RAF Akrotiri, Cyprus – taking advantage of the fine Mediterranean weather – something that has been repeated annually since. In early 1980, the team was given official permission for its own squadron badge, featuring a Diamond Nine formation and the motto 'Éclat' ('Brilliance'). The Red Arrows flew their first Hawk public display in the UK at Sywell on 6 April and completed 119 shows by the end of the season.

On 17 May 1980, the team suffered its first Hawk write-off when the pilot struck the mast of a moving yacht during a display along the seafront at Brighton. Sqn Ldr Steve Johnson was able to eject before the aircraft (XX262) crashed into the sea. No blame was attached to the pilot but the incident did lead to a subsequent ban on all displays flying below 100ft (30m).

A new home at Scampton

The Red Arrows left Kemble for the last time on 10 March 1983 when the team flew to Akrotiri for winter training. They returned to the UK on 5 April and made their new home at RAF Scampton, Lincolnshire. In May, the team embarked on its second tour of Canada and the USA, retracing many of the steps flown by the 1972 team. The 100th anniversary of manned flight was being marked at the Andrews Air Force Base Armed Force Day and a crowd of over 700,000 watched the team's 20-minute show – to rave reviews. The team flew back to Scampton on 27 May, having completed 400 hours flying during the three-and-half-week tour, enhancing the Hawk's reputation for serviceability and demonstrating to its NATO allies that British technology and training were among the best in the world.

A significant milestone for the team was reached when the team flew its 2,000th public display, at Bournemouth Airport, on 1 June 1986. Two weeks later, the team departed on a 17-nation tour of the Far East. During the six-week trip, the team established new records for itself and the BAe Hawk, travelling some 18,800 miles (30,255km) and completing 22 displays, without any cancellations due to bad weather or aircraft unserviceability.

Sadly, further accidents occurred during the winter training practice for the 1988 season, when two Hawks collided near Scampton. Both pilots ejected but were injured; Sqn Ldr Miller suffered back injuries and was able to return to the team after a few weeks, but Flt Lt Spike

The Red Arrows took delivery of the first Hawk T1 (XX251) at RAF Bitteswell on 16 August 1979 while the ninth Hawk was received on 29 October 1979. The 'last' Hawk (XX266) was handed over at Bitteswell on 15 November 1979. To celebrate the arrival of the first aircraft, XX251 led a nine-aircraft formation of Red Arrows' Gnats over RAF Kemble. (Crown Copyright)

To mark the team's official 40th display season in 1994, a private event was organised at RAF Cranwell on 21 May in which a privately owned Folland Gnat (G-BVPP/XP534) painted as 'XR993' with Sqn Ldr Willie Hackett at the controls, flew the first manoeuvre in formation with the Red Arrows team. At the 50th Anniversary Airshow for the College of Aeronautics at Cranfield on 8 June 1996, 11 Red Arrows' Hawk T1a, were lined up alongside the Gnat T1 'XR993' on the ramp prior to the flying display. The event was not repeated for the public. (Peter R March)

Newberry was treated for a broken leg and was replaced on the team by Flt Lt Dom Riley. Two months later, on 22 January 1988, Flt Lt Neil MacLachan was killed during a low-level formation training flight. His place on the team was taken by Sqn Ldr Jeff Glover. A further accident occurred when, on 24 June 1988, Sqn Ldr Pete Collins ejected on take-off at Scampton in XX304 and was seriously injured. The team had no time to train a replacement and so was reduced to a seven-ship display for the remainder of the year.

Anniversary roll

To mark the Red Arrows' 25th anniversary, 1989 saw a return to nine aircraft and the introduction of several new manoeuvres, including the Big Vixen Roll; 101 displays were flown.

In June of the following year, the team made an historic visit to the Soviet Union where it flew two displays over the Ukrainian capital, Kiev, in support of the British Trade Fair.

The team flew its 3,000th display at the official opening of the Dartmouth Royal Regatta on 23 August 1995. With the end of the Cold War, Scampton fell victim to the government's defence cuts and was closed at the end of the year. The team departed on an unprecedented five-month, 50,000-mile (80,465km) tour of South Africa, Australia and the Far East in September. The tour, sponsored by ten major British companies, routed through 23 countries in the Middle East and Africa. Among several firsts was a visit to South Africa where the team performed in celebrations to mark the 75th anniversary of the South African Air Force.

The second part of the tour took the team through the Middle East and southern and southeast Asia. It displayed at the Malaysian International Air Show – LIMA 95 – at Langkawi. In mid-January, the team arrived in Australia where it performed over Sydney Harbour in front of an estimated 1.2 million people. Next were displays in Brunei and the Philippines before it performed at the Asian Aerospace 1996 Air Show in Singapore. En route to the UK, the team displayed in Bangkok before returning to its new home at RAF Cranwell, Lincolnshire, on 21 February 1996. The significance and success of this gruelling five-month trip can be seen when one considers the countries that subsequently ordered the Hawk aircraft.

In November 1999, they departed on another tour of the Middle and Far East. The six-week deployment saw the Red Arrows appearing at the opening of LIMA 99 (the Langkawi International Maritime and Aerospace Exhibition) in Malaysia and at the Dubai 2000 International Air Show.

After moving to Cranwell in 1996, the team was able to retain the use of Scampton for winter training due to the intensity of flying already at Cranwell. However, with a further review of flying training, the team returned to Scampton on 21 December 2000, with supervision and support provided by Cranwell.

⋀ **Although painted in Red Arrows' colours, XM708 was a standard trainer – known as a Tin Ship – that is, it was not modified with smoke-making equipment and had only a UHF radio. It was the unofficial 11th aircraft and belonged to 4 FTS/CFS. After being withdrawn from service the aircraft was allocated the maintenance serial 8573M when transferred as an instructional airframe to RAF Halton. It was photographed at an Open Day in the 1980s.** *(Keith Wilson)*

August 2002 saw the team deploy briefly to Canada but this led to the cancellation of 14 shows in the UK. One of the seasons many highlights was the formation flypast with Concorde (G-BOAD) over Buckingham Palace during the Queen's Jubilee Celebrations on 4 June.

Celebrating 4,000 displays

The team's 2006 display season began with a three-week goodwill tour of the Far East, Middle East and Europe. Designed to promote British industry, the tour visited eight countries, including Jordan, India, Oman, Abu Dhabi, Bahrain, Saudi Arabia, Greece and Spain. The short tour was an amazing commercial success. Other memorable highlights from the year included the team's participation in the Queen's Birthday flypast on 17 June when it formed part of a mass formation of Typhoon, Tornado and Jaguar fighters that overflew London, as well as the teams' 4,000th official display at the RAF Leuchars show on 9 September.

To coincide with a six-week tour of the Middle and Far East in November 2007, the team unveiled a new paint scheme – the first since the Hawk aircraft were delivered to the Red Arrows in 1979. The new scheme featured the title 'Royal Air Force' in white along the fuselage and was designed to remind its audience of the team's pride in representing the Royal Air Force. The tour was supported by Rolls-Royce and BAe Systems and the Red Arrows visited 13 countries and flew 15,000 miles (24,140 km) before returning to the UK on 18 December.

In May 2009, it was announced that Kirsty Moore (now Stewart) had been selected as the first woman pilot to fly in the Red Arrows team since its formation in 1965.

The team suffered a setback in March 2010 when two aircraft collided over Kastelli, Crete, during pre-season training. Flt Lt Ling was able to eject from his Hawk (XX233) but suffered injuries serious enough to prevent him flying for the remainder of the season. He was replaced by Sqn Ldr Paul O'Grady, who rejoined the team at short notice. The other aircraft involved in the collision was flown by Flt Lt David Montenegro, who landed his Hawk (XX253) safely, despite the damage. The incident delayed the team's training and a revised schedule was devised with the team making its first public appearance in June, when it took part in the Queen's Birthday flypast, followed by shows at Brize Norton and Cosford.

The year 2011 was particularly difficult for the team. On 7 August, while displaying at the end of a show along Blackpool's seafront, Red 7 (XX260) took a bird strike which caused significant engine and fuselage damage. Flt Lt Ben Plank managed to get the aircraft safely onto the runway at the nearby Blackpool Airport. With high airframe hours and fatigue index, it was decided to permanently withdraw the aircraft from service and it was removed to RAF Shawbury by road.

After completing a show at the Bournemouth Air Festival, along the seafront, the team returned to Bournemouth Airport. Tragically, Red 7, flown by Flt Lt Jon Egging, flew into the ground and the pilot was killed. As a result of this, as yet, unexplained crash, the Red Arrows were grounded while an inquiry took place before the team returned to the air as an eight-ship formation to complete the 2011 schedule. On 27 September, after making a final appearance at Ostrava, they returned to Scampton having completed 69 displays during the season.

The team took a customary short break and then started working up for the 2012 season with four new members, including a new team leader, Sqn Ldr Jim Turner. Unusually kind autumn weather had ensured that practice was progressing well when tragedy struck again. On 8 November, Flt Lt Sean Cunningham was killed when he was ejected from his aircraft while on

the ramp at Scampton. A full Service Inquiry was set up to investigate the circumstances and all Hawk jets throughout the RAF were grounded, pending the outcome. Not only were the Reds unable to practise, but the aircraft were not made available to the maintenance team for the all-important winter servicing programme, crucial to the overall success of the team.

On 8 December 2011 it was announced that 'sufficient technical and safety advice has been provided to allow the MoD to release all Hawk T. Mk.1A aircraft, including those of The Red Arrows, back into service'. Following a short period of staff continuation training, the Reds resumed display training for the 2012 season.

It was simultaneously announced that Sqn Ldr Martin Higgins – initially invited back to the team as Red 10 – would assume the role of Red 5. Higgins had previously served with the team from 2004 to 2007 as Red 3 and 9 and this previous experience was considered essential in the decision.

Another 'old boy' – Sqn Ldr Martin Ling – was invited back to take up the role as Red 10. Ling had previously operated as Red 3 in 2008, Red 7 in 2009 and was to fly as Red 6 in 2010 before the unfortunate accident at Kastelli, Crete, in March 2010 had prevented this.

By early 2012 the team was significantly behind with its training programme as a result of the loss of Sean Cunningham, followed by serious delays in the winter maintenance programme. Poor weather in January and February further hindered matters while the members were working towards the award of their Public Display Authority for the 2012 season. Then in March the RAF announced that the Reds would display with seven aircraft rather than the usual nine during 2012 due to the unavoidable posting of Kirsty Stewart during the annual winter training period. Acknowledging that 2012 would be a highly significant year, the RAF confirmed that key flypast engagements – notably the Queen's Diamond Jubilee and the opening ceremony of the London Olympic Games – would be flown by nine aircraft. They also gave reassurance that the reduction to seven aircraft for 2012 was a one-off and the team would return to its full complement of nine aircraft and pilots for 2013.

➤ **The Red Arrows' HQ at RAF Scampton is 'guarded' by Gnat T1 XR571 – an aircraft that despite its colour scheme, did not serve with the Red Arrows.**
(Keith Wilson)

the People

What makes a great team? The Oxford English Dictionary definition is 'to come together as a team to achieve a shared goal'. Simply stated, it is less 'me' and more 'we'. The Red Arrows are a great team; despite all the competition out there they are probably the best fast jet aerobatic display team in the world and that did not happen by accident. It is all about the sum of the individuals – teamwork.

The Red Arrows are the Royal Air Force Aerobatic Team (RAFAT). All members of the team are RAF personnel – all having served on operations overseas before volunteering to join the team. The command structure is similar to other RAF squadrons.

◁ **An unofficial picture of the 2011 Red Arrows taken at RAF Scampton on 5 August 2011, shortly after an In Season Practice (ISP) and before they departed to Bournemouth. Left to right: Sqn Ldr Graeme Bagnall (Red 10), Flt Lt Dave Davies (Red 8), Flt Lt Jon Egging (Red 4), Flt Lt Chris Lyndon-Smith (Red 2), Sqn Ldr Ben Murphy (Red 1), Flt Lt Sean Cunningham (Red 3), Flt Lt Zane Sennett (Red 9), Flt Lt David Montenegro (Red 6), Flt Lt Kirsty Stewart (Red 5) and Flt Lt Ben Plank (Red 7).**
(Oliver Wilson)

A Sqn Ldr Ben Murphy, Officer
Commanding RAFAT and Red
Arrows team leader (Red 1) for 2010
and 2011. Ben also flew with the Red
Arrows in 2007 (Red 2), 2008 (Red 7)
and 2009 (Red 6) before being
promoted and posted as team leader
for 2010/11. *(Keith Wilson)*

➢ Flt Lt Chris
Lyndon-Smith joined
the Red Arrows in
2011 and flew as Red
2. In 2012, he will be
flying as Red 7 – one
half of the Synchro
Pair. *(Keith Wilson)*

Red 1 – the Squadron Commander

The Squadron Commander, also known as Red 1 reports to the
Commandant of the Central Flying School through Red 11, the team's
Senior Flying Supervisor and Officer Commanding Operations Wing at
RAF Scampton. The post of Red 1 is not advertised and applications
are not accepted. Instead, the post is appointed by the Air Officer
Commanding (AOC) 22 (Training) Group and endorsed by the Chief
of the Air Staff (CAS). They will consult with the desk officers at Air
Command as to who is likely to be available and suitably qualified
(have been a Red Arrows' display pilot previously and carrying the
substantive rank of Squadron Leader) and invite/offer the suitable
candidate the appointment. It is the only post within the Red Arrows
where there is no selection procedure to endure. For 2010 and 2011,
the team was led by Sqn Ldr Ben Murphy. Ben had previously served
with the team in 2007 (as Red 2), 2008 (as Red 7) and 2009 (as Red
6). Normally, the post is for three years but somewhat unusually Ben
had completed five years in succession with the Reds. At the end of the
2011 season, he stood down before moving on to a new task.

The post was then offered to Sqn Ldr Jim Turner. Once again, Jim
had previously served with the team in 2005 (as Red 5), 2006 (as
Red 7) and 2007 (as Red 6) before taking up a role in Saudi Arabia
as team adviser to the Royal Saudi Air Force display team – the
Saudi Hawks.

⋀ Flt Lt Jon Egging joined the Red Arrows in 2011 and flew as Red 4. Jon was tragically killed when his Hawk T1 crashed around half a mile south-east of Bournemouth Airport on 20 August 2011, shortly after the Red Arrows had completed a display along Bournemouth seafront.
(Keith Wilson)

⟋ The first female team member, Flt Lt Kirsty Stewart, joined the Red Arrows in 2010 and flew as Red 3. In 2011 she flew as Red 5 and in 2012 she is flying as Red 9, as well as serving as the team's Executive Officer.
(Crown Copyright/SAC Rob Travis)

⋘ Flt Lt Sean Cunningham joined the Red Arrows in 2011 and flew as Red 3. He was due to fly as Red 5 in the 2012 line-up but was tragically killed at RAF Scampton on the morning of 8 November 2011 when he was ejected from his Hawk aircraft, XX177. He was photographed on the Red Arrows' stand at the Royal International Air Tattoo (RIAT) on 17 July 2011.
(Keith Wilson)

➢ Flt Lt David Montenegro joined the Red Arrows in 2009 when he flew as Red 3. In 2010, he moved to the Red 7 position and in 2011 – his last year with the team –David flew as Red 6, the Synchro leader.
(Keith Wilson)

➤ **Flt Lt Ben Plank** joined the Red Arrows in 2010 and initially flew as Red 2. In 2011 he moved into the Red 7 slot (as Synchro 2) and in 2012 will be Red 6 – the Synchro leader. *(Crown Copyright/ SAC Rob Travis)*

⋀ **Flt Lt Zane Sennett** joined the Red Arrows in 2009 and initially flew as Red 2. In 2010, Zane moved into the Red 5 slot before taking up the role of Red 9 in 2011, his final year with the team. After leaving the Reds, Zane transferred to the Royal Australian Air Force where he flies the FA-18. Zane was photographed at Airbourne 2011, Eastbourne, in August 2011, signing autographs for visitors. *(Keith Wilson)*

◄ **Flt Lt Dave Davies** joined the Red Arrows in 2009 and initially flew as Red 4. In 2010 he retained that position before moving to Red 8 in 2011, as well as being the Squadron Executive Officer. David was photographed at Airbourne 2011, Eastbourne, in August 2011, signing autographs for the audience. *(Keith Wilson)*

⋀ Sqn Ldr Graeme
Bagnall joined the Red
Arrows in 2009 as Red 10
– the team manager – a
role he served in for three
years. Graeme has been
posted to Nevada in a new
role with the RAF.
*(Crown Copyright/SAC Dan
Herrick)*

⭧ A new recruit to the
Red Arrows was Sqn Ldr
Ross Priday, who joined
the team in 2011 as the
Senior Engineering Officer
(SEngO), one of only 13
team members permitted
to wear the special red
flying suits. Ross was
photographed at
Airbourne 2011,
Eastbourne in August
2011, signing autographs
for the audience.
(Keith Wilson)

➢ Another newcomer to
the Red Arrows in 2011
was Flt Lt Adam Littler,
who joined as the team's
Junior Engineering Officer
(JEngO). In addition to
being the squadron's
JEngO, Adam also holds
the post of Circus 1 and
although wearing the
famous red flying suit, he
leads the very special
Circus team of blue-
overalled engineers who
fly in the back seats of the
jets. *(Keith Wilson)*

The Reds' selection process

For the remaining, highly sought-after positions, individuals must volunteer and apply. Normally, three new team members are recruited each year and occupy positions two, three and four within the diamond formation – flying within the front Enid section of the formation. Applications are usually received before the end of the year and to apply each candidate needs to satisfy three key criteria.

They must:

• be fast jet pilots with a minimum of 1,500 hours

• have completed an operational tour

• have been graded as 'above average' during their flying career

Around 35 applications are received annually, normally from pilots with at least 12 years in service.

Sqn Ldr Murphy took the author through the selection process:

I receive and review all the applicants' Flying Reports, including training and frontline tours. Their individual traits are noted and then – anonymously – are presented to the rest of the team. Each application is categorised as an A, B, C or D, with 'A' being the most likely to succeed. Once this has been completed by all of the team members, we bring in the names of individuals and reflect on our choices. We select nine candidates and invite them to join us in Cyprus for Exercise Springhawk for one week in the following March or April. Here, they each fly three backseat rides a day, just as we do, during the working-up period. They socialise with us throughout the week and then have a 30-minute interview followed by an individual 15–20-minute flying test, usually with the team's Executive Officer, involving lots of rolls and loops.

Is it not difficult to confirm an applicant's suitability from such a relatively short flying test? 'You can usually tell immediately,' says Murphy. 'They are on a very sharp learning curve and how they handle that learning curve is important to us; as is their smooth handling of the jet as well as error analysis.'

If they get this far, they can expect a PR interview at which some very tricky questions are posed. 'Once all that is completed, all nine of us get into a room along with our Senior Engineering Officer (SEngO), Team Manager and PR staff to decide who will get the call,' says Murphy. 'It is important we satisfy ourselves that whoever gets the call must be able to fly very well, fit in and work as a team player – the chemistry is everything!'

It is not just the pilots who have to go through this demanding process; any post that carries a Red flying suit will also have to endure it, including the Team Manager, SEngO, Junior Engineering Officer (JEngO) and the Road Manager (Red 10), although these posts are not required to do the flying test and the latter post does not go through the shortlist process in Cyprus.

The official Reds' team image for 2011 taken at Scampton in March 2011. Front row, left to right: Flt Lt Adam Littler (JEngO), Sqn Ldr Ross Priday (SEngO), Sqn Ldr Liz Parker (team manager), Sqn Leader Ben Murphy (Red 1), Flt Lt Chris Lyndon-Smith (Red 2), Flt Lt Sean Cunningham (Red 3), Flt Lt Jon Egging (Red 4) and Flt Lt Kirsty Stewart (Red 5). Back row, on the wing: Sqn Ldr Graeme Bagnall (Red 10), Flt Lt Zane Sennett (Red 9), Flt Lt David Davies (Red 8), Flt Lt Ben Plank (Red 7), Flt Lt David Montenegro (Red 6). *(Crown Copyright/SAC Rob Travis)*

The Engineering Team

The Red Arrows' Engineering Team is led by the SEngO, Sqn Ldr Ross Priday, who is responsible for all engineering and logistical matters. Ross's role has particular emphasis on strategic maintenance matters, including the winter service programme for the team jets. The SEngO tour is usually for two years, although Ross is very keen to extend that time so that he can see through a number of major projects, including the Hawk Replacement Programme.

Ross heads an engineering team – the 'Blues' because of the blue overalls they wear – consisting of around 80 engineers, including mechanical, avionics, weapons, mechanical transport, survival equipment and supply specialists. Mechanical Technicians make up around 60% of the Red Arrows' Engineering Team and are responsible for the maintenance and rectification of the airframes and engines on the team's Hawk aircraft.

Flt Sgt Steve Cox is the Senior 'Engineering' Blue and is responsible for the management, discipline and welfare of the Blues. Known affectionately as the squadron's 'Rottweiler', Steve joined the RAF in 1978 and trained as a propulsion technician, specialising in aircraft engines, and since then has built up a wealth of knowledge and experience. Steve's work within the RAF, and especially with the Red Arrows, was recognised when he was awarded an AOC Commendation in the 2011 New Year's Honours.

Ross is supported by the JEngO, Flt Lt Adam Littler, who also operates as Circus 1. Adam's role is generally tactical – he runs the flightline and the Circus, the small team of engineers who fly in the back seat of the jets to all the shows and events. As Circus 1, Adam always sits behind Red 1. While 'on the road', Adam is responsible for the safety and welfare of the Circus, as well as all Standards and Practices activities and engineering documentation. Adam applied for the JEngO post when he saw it advertised and went through a full two-day selection process. While the final decision falls to Red 1 and the SEngO, all the engineering team have an input, including the SACs. For Adam it was a dream role: 'It offers all the usual JEngO opportunities with lots more responsibility. It allows many opportunities to represent both the Royal Air Force and your country; and to work with a great team of highly motivated individuals. And you get to fly in the back of a Red Arrows' jet!'

➤ **The official Blues image for 2011, taken on the ramp at RAF Scampton, March 2011.** (Crown Copyright/SAC Rob Travis)

⋀ Cpl Kev Smith is an avionics technician who was posted to the Red Arrows in 2009. He was a member of the Reserve Circus in 2010; in 2011 Kev was appointed as Circus 5 and flew with Red 5, Flt Lt Kirsty Stewart. In addition, Kev was Deputy Circus Leader for 2011.
(Keith Wilson)

➤ The 2011 Blues at work on the ramp at Scampton in August 2011, while preparing the team for an ISP prior to a four-day push to Bournemouth, Aldergrove and Hawarden.
(Keith Wilson)

∧ When the Blues are in the back seats of the jets, the Reserve Circus step into their shoes and prepare the jets for departure – as they did at Scampton on 5 August 2011, when the team were involved in a push to Bournemouth, Aldergrove and Hawarden. *(Keith Wilson)*

➤ Hawk XX264 underwent maintenance during the mid-season break at Scampton in July 2011 with three AMM technicians allocated to complete the various tasks: SAC Lawrence Strachan, SAC Phil Broadbent and SAC James Mitchell. *(Keith Wilson)*

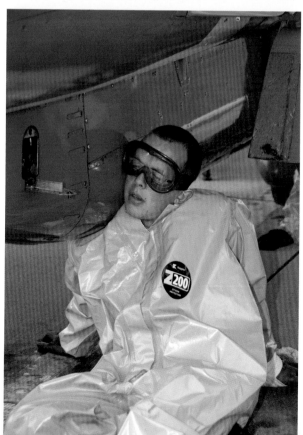

➤ SAC Jason Stanway was a member of the 2011 Dye Team and was photographed in protective clothing at Scampton on 3 July 2011 while preparing the jets for a display at RAF Waddington. He keeps one ear on the diesel and dye pod to hear when the various compartments are full, and to prevent surplus dye running out onto the ramp. *(Keith Wilson)*

➤➤ Three members of the Red Arrows' ground engineering team working on the starboard main undercarriage leg of a Hawk jet at Scampton: SAC Maria Cowie, SAC James Smith and SAC James Mitchell. *(Keith Wilson)*

➤ **Leading the team of three photographers at RAF Scampton is Cpl Graham Taylor. He was photographed recording the ISP at Scampton on 5 August 2011. Without one of the team on the ground, videoing every manoeuvre, the display cannot take place. The team is also responsible for most of its stills photography.**
(Keith Wilson)

∨ **The Red Arrows' photographic team at Scampton in December 2011, suitably protected against the elements. Left to right: SAC Dan Herrick, Cpl Graham and SAC Rob Travis.**
(Crown Copyright/ Flt Lt Al Mundy)

Team Manager

The Red Arrows' Team Manager for 2011 and 2012 is Sqn Ldr Liz Parker. Liz joined the Royal Air Force in 1991 after starting her career in the Army. She completed the Joint Air Traffic Control Course at RAF Cranwell before gaining all her ATC operating endorsements. Liz has been posted overseas on many occasions. The first was to Hungary on Operation Deny Flight, controlling NATO E-3 assets over Bosnia. Shortly afterwards she was posted to the Falkland Islands – the first of three tours to the islands. In 2005/6 she was detached to Iraq in support of Operation TELIC. On her return she was appointed as the acting Senior Air Traffic Control Office (SATCO) at RAF Shawbury.

At very short notice in December 2009, Liz was detached to Afghanistan in support of Operation HERRICK to provide specialist advice and control of the increasingly busy airspace over Helmand Province. Based at Camp Bastion, she was the coalition airspace coordinator for Operation MOSHTARAK – the largest UK aerial assault since the Second World War.

Liz is in her second year as Team Manager and runs a very tight ship. That said, she is a great hands-on manager who leads by example. During the season you will often find her in her red flying suit at many of the major shows coordinating all the PR and sponsor activities, while in the winter months she often conducts the weekly Red Arrows' tour parties at RAF Scampton. Liz is also at the forefront of much the team's charity work and is an executor of the Red Arrows Charitable Trust.

Team Adjutant

The Team Adjutant is WO Alan Murray. Alan joined the RAF in 1970 as a Clerk Secretarial apprentice. His first overseas posting was to Episkopi, Cyprus, in 1974. However, within four weeks his dream posting changed dramatically with the coup and subsequent invasion of the island. Alan has completed three tours in Germany including a four-year stint in the British Embassy in Bonn, serving as the assistant to the Air Attaché.

Alan controls the purse strings for much of the team's expenditure, including its travel and subsistence costs. He is probably best known for his planning skills and amazing attention to detail. He produces the weekly WHAM (What's Happening Manager) planning schedule (see Chapter 6) around which the team operates – in fact it is central to their *modi operandi*.

◁ **The Red Arrows' Team Manager for 2011 and 2012 is Squadron Leader Liz Parker. Liz joined the Royal Air Force in 1991 after starting her career in the Army. She is a great hands-on manager who leads by example. During the season you will often find her in her red flying suit at many of the major shows co-ordinating the PR and sponsor activities, while in the winter months she often conducts the weekly Red Arrows' tour parties at RAF Scampton. Liz is also heavily involved in much the Team's charity work and is an executor of the Red Arrows Charitable Trust.** *(Crown Copyright/SAC Rob Travis)*

⋁ **The Team Adjutant is Warrant Office Alan Murray, BEM. Alan controls the purse strings for much of the Team's expenditure, although he is probably best known for his planning skills and amazing attention to detail. He produces the weekly WHAM? planning schedules around which the team operates.** *(Crown Copyright/SAC Rob Travis)*

One of the Red Arrows' greatest fans is William Mansell, a special needs young man who has been following the team since he first saw them at Mildenhall when he was just ten years old. He got a chance to meet them in the Breitling chalet at RIAT in July 2011, when he was able to get this 'special' picture with Flt Lt Kirsty Stewart (Red 5) and Flt Lt Zane Sennett (Red 9).
(Keith Wilson)

After having spent time in the Red Arrows' chalet at RIAT in July 2011, some of the team visited the Royal Air Force Association (RAFA) chalet to continue signing autographs and meeting the public face-to-face. Flt Lts Jon Egging (Red 4) and Chris Lyndon-Smith (Red 2) were photographed signing autographs on 17 July 2011 ahead of the team's display in the afternoon.
(Keith Wilson)

The Red Arrows' chalet at RIAT in July 2011. Meeting the public are (left to right) Flt Lt Chris Lyndon-Smith (Red 2), Flt Lt Jon Egging (Red 4), Sqn Ldr Ben Murphy (Red 1), Flt Lt Kirsty Stewart and Flt Lt Sean Cunningham (Red 3).
(Keith Wilson)

Another view at RIAT in July 2011. To the left is Sqn Ldr Ben Murphy (Red 1) and to the right is Flt Lt Sean Cunningham (Red 3) signing a small team brochure for one of the queuing public. The chalet was busy throughout the day while members of the team were on duty. *(Keith Wilson)*

Three young fans of the Red Arrows await the signatures of Sqn Ldr Ben Murphy (Red 1), Flt Jon Egging (Red 4) and Flt Lt Chris Lyndon-Smith (Red 2) at the RAFA chalet at RIAT in July 2011. *(Keith Wilson)*

A Red Arrows' pilot of the future? Six-year-old Morgan Howcroft met the team at a show in 2010. Afterwards he decided that he too wanted to be a Red Arrows' pilot. He collected the signatures of most of the 2011 team while visiting the RAFA chalet at Fairford in July 2010, where he is proudly showing them to SAC Gemma Somerfield, a member of the Red Arrows' PR team. *(Keith Wilson)*

Most people want the Red Arrows' brochures or caps signed, but these young Turkish women at the Izmir Airshow on 16 June 2011 prefer to collect the team signatures on their arms. Flt Lt Chris Lyndon-Smith (Red 2) obliges. *(Crown Copyright/ Cpl Graham Taylor)*

Flt Lt Zane Sennett (Red 9) with Councillor Carolyn Heaps, Mayor of Eastbourne, at the town's Airbourne 2011 seafront event in July 2011. *(Keith Wilson)*

The People

Supporting charities

You may be forgiven for thinking that with all the activities involved in making the Red Arrows happen, nobody would have time for other activities outside the squadron. However, the team assists more than 500 charitable causes a year by donating raffle and auction items. In 2010, they helped to raise thousands of pounds for the Royal Air Forces Association by taking part in the London Marathon when Sqn Ldr Ben Murphy, accompanied by Reds 2 to 10, completed the course.

At the end of the 2010 display season, the pilots and some of the support staff joined forces with their display colleagues from the Battle of Britain Memorial Flight (BBMF) to travel from Land's End to John O'Groats on Vespa scooters, to raise money for a variety of causes, including Help for Heroes, Fly2Help, Whizz-Kidz, The Royal Air Force Benevolent Fund and the Royal Air Forces Association.

A year later, at the end of 2011, the team once again joined forces with the BBMF and completed a 400-mile cycle ride from the westernmost point on the UK mainland to the most easterly. The '400in4' trip covered the 400 miles in just four days. Sadly, the event took place without Flt Lt Jon Egging, but his place on the trip was taken by his wife Dr Emma Egging. It had been hoped to raise £50,000, to be split equally between the RAF Wings Appeal and Fly2Help. In the end the trip raised more than £79,000 and the surplus of £29,000 was donated to the Jon Egging Trust.

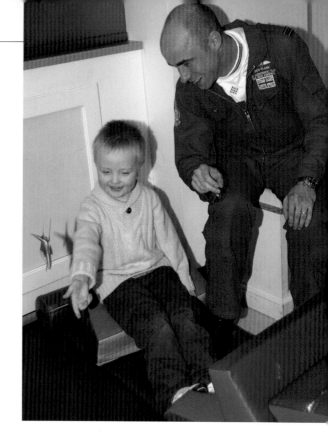

◄ One of the young children being visited at the Great Ormond Street Hospital in December 2011 is 5-year-old David, who receives an impromptu flying lesson from Red 6, Flt Lt Ben Plank. *(Keith Wilson)*

➤ Seven members of the Red Arrows at the Great Ormond Street Hospital in December 2011. The team split into two groups to visit as many of the wards and facilities as possible. The four children entertaining the team in The Centre are, left to right: Reet, Amelia, David and Johney. *(Keith Wilson)*

∇ '400in4', the Jon Egging Coast to Coast Challenge. On 11 October 2011, a combined team of 23 cyclists from the Red Arrows, the RAF's Battle of Britain Memorial Flight, and Fly2Help charity set off to cross the UK at its widest point in just four days. The route began at St David's Head in Wales and finished in Lowestoft, Suffolk, with the cyclists riding approximately 100 miles (160km) a day. The project was hoping to raise around £50,000, with the proceeds being split equally between the Royal Air Force Association and the Fly2help scheme. By the end of the trip the sum raised reached £79,000 and it was agreed to donate the final £29,000 to the Jon Egging Memorial Trust. The successful cyclists were photographed at Lowestoft on the completion of the trip on 14 October. *(Crown Copyright/SAC Rob Travis)*

The Red Arrows' trademarks – Diamond Nine and associated logos – earn money for the Red Arrows Charitable Trust through royalties. Once a year the cash, usually in the region of £40,000, is distributed to various good causes. All funds are bid for, but the executors tend to target the smaller charities where a small amount of money can have a significant impact on its activities.

Subject to flying commitments, the Red Arrows allow a small group of visitors (12 to 15 people) to visit Scampton every Wednesday and spend a day with the Reds. Most are winners of raffles and auctions conducted by charities supported by the Reds; all have a great day out.

Once a year, just before the Christmas break, team members don their red flying suits and pay a visit to the Great Ormond Street Hospital for Children (GOSH) in London. For some members it is probably the first time they have worn their red suit in public and very often the last time before the team earns the right to wear them once the Public Display Authority has been awarded in the spring. Such is the demand for their time at GOSH that the team members divide into two groups and tour as many wards and facilities as possible. Wherever they visit small crowds gather and the impact they have on staff and parents is extraordinary to witness.

The Red Arrows is a very special Team. During the course of 2011, tragedy struck not once, but twice, and the members' resilience in dealing with both incidents showed both character and inner strength – individually and collectively.

Nine pilots, 60 engineers, 47 years flying and more than 4,400 displays – the headlines are simple and impressive, the facts speak for themselves.

What makes this special Team so special? Each Team member is a volunteer. Each Team member is a key player. But it is the teamwork that makes it special. The Red Arrows represent teamwork personified.

The 2012 team

For the 2012 season the Reds will display with seven aircraft rather than the usual nine.

Red 1	Sqn Ldr Jim Turner (OC RAFAT)
Red 2	Flt Lt Martin Pert
Red 3	Flt Lt Mike Child
Red 4	Flt Lt James McMillan
Red 5	Sqn Ldr Martin Higgins (Executive Officer)
Red 6	Flt Lt Ben Plank (Synchro leader)
Red 7	Flt Lt Chris Lyndon-Smith
Red 8	Flt Lt Dave Davies
Red 10	Sqn Ldr Mike Ling
Team Manager	Sqn Ldr Liz Parker
SEngO	Sqn Ldr Ross Priday
JEngO	Flt Lt Adam Littler (Circus 1)
Team Adjutant	WO Alan Murray BEM
Circus 1	JEngO Flt Lt Adam Littler (flying with Red 1)
Circus 2	SAC Glenn Jones (flying with Red 2)
Circus 3	SAC Nick Williams (flying with Red 3)
Circus 4	Cpl Lyndon Picken (flying with Red 4)
Circus 5	Sgt Tim Elton (Circus Leader) (Flying with Red 5)
Circus 6	SAC Glynn West (Flying with Red 6)
Circus 7	Cpl Jamie Hatcher (Flying with Red 7)
Circus 8	Cpl Lee Barnes (Flying with Red 8)
Circus 10	SAC Simon Watkins (Flying with Red 10)

Every Christmas, the Red Arrows make a visit to Great Ormond Street Hospital for Children. The team, dressed in their red uniforms, was photographed alongside the Peter Pan statue outside the hospital entrance on 15 December 2011. *(Keith Wilson)*

The Red Arrows' Gnat T1s in the Viggen nine-ship formation – new for the 1975 season. This formation has been used by the team on numerous occasions and featured in the 2011 programme. *(Crown Copyright)*

A competition was launched on the BBC children's television programme *Blue Peter* to name a new formation for the Red Arrows. The winner was 'Angel of the North', since renamed the Lancaster, and the formation was incorporated into the 2000 display. *(Crown Copyright)*

word 'Éclat', meaning brilliance. Diamond Nine is almost exclusively flown in a bend, but is also seen as a logical step between other formations. Perhaps the best use of the Diamond Nine was in the 2000 programme when it followed an Eagle Quarter Clover, when both sides of the formation moved forward from that formation into Diamond Nine.

A role for each Red

Each member of the team has their own position within each formation and, effectively, they all follow the leader. Red 6 would appear to have the easiest job in the nine-ship formations flown during the first half of the display, as the aircraft is normally positioned directly behind the leader. However, Red 6 is also the Synchro leader in the second half of the display, along with the significant additional responsibilities that accompany that task. Reds 2 and 3 would normally sit either side of the leader. The situation is a little more difficult for Reds 4, 5, 7, 8 and 9 as they will usually have another aircraft sitting between them and the leader so picking the formation reference is not as easy. Usually, this is accomplished by taking a reference from the leader as well as another reference from the aircraft closest to them. The logic applied to the numbering system in all formations remains the same, with even numbers to the right of the leader and odd numbers to the left. The lower numbers, usually the newer members of the team, are closer to the front.

The first half of the display consists of a series of loops and rolls, along with manoeuvres such as the quarter clover, rollback, barrel roll and hesitation roll. Each of them requires a particular skill, especially when flown in very close formation as the Red Arrows do.

The Programme

➤ The classic Red Arrows' entry from behind the crowd line, as seen at the Royal International Air Tattoo (RIAT) at Fairford on 17 July 2011, at the start of the team's Rolling Display owing to the day's relatively low cloud base. *(Oliver Wilson)*

ᐯ As the team passes overhead, above the crowd line, the outside two aircraft roll, a manoeuvre known as 9-Arrow to Fred, seen at another Rolling Display, this time the Lowestoft seafront event on 12 August 2011. *(Keith Wilson)*

➤ In the Full Display sequence, after the team has entered from behind the crowd, it starts to climb with the aircraft top sides towards the public; the aircraft move from Fred to Short Diamond Twist, in anticipation of looping over the top of the manoeuvre, as they are doing at the Cromer Carnival on 17 August 2011, followed by the Short Diamond Twist Roll. *(Both, Keith Wilson)*

◄ If the team is performing a Rolling or Flat Display due to the limited cloud ceiling, the manoeuvre becomes the Short Diamond Bend, as performed at the RIAT on 17 July 2011. *(Keith Wilson)*

▽ The Big Vixen Roll can be performed in both the Full and Rolling Display sequence, but changes to Big Vixen Reversal for the Flat Display. At the Cromer Carnival on 17 August 2011, Red 1 is flying a non-smoking black Hawk T1, XX284, during the display. *(Keith Wilson)*

➤ From the Big Vixen Roll, the team moves through 9-Arrow before forming the swan shape for the graceful Swan Loop manoeuvre, as seen during the Full Display at the cliff-top Cromer Carnival show in 2011. *(Keith Wilson)*

Weather-dependent displays

The Red Arrows practise and then receive a Public Display Authority (PDA) for three different weather-dependent displays – the Full Display, Rolling Display and Flat Display. To carry out a full looping display, the base of the cloud must be above 4,500ft (1,372m) to avoid the aircraft entering cloud at the top of a loop. If the cloud base is less than 4,500ft (1,372m) but greater than 2,500ft (762m), the team will perform the Rolling Display, when they substitute wing-over and rolling manoeuvres for the loops normally flown in the Full Display. If the cloud base is less than 2,500ft (762m), they will fly the Flat Display, which consists of a series of flypasts and steep turns in a variety of formations and shapes, keeping the team clear of the cloud base.

Sqn Ldr Ben Murphy flew with the Red Arrows for five years: firstly as Red 2 in 2007, then as Red 7 in 2008 before taking up the Red 6 slot in 2009. He was then appointed Team Leader (Red 1) for both 2010 and 2011. Flying with the team for five years is not unusual, but doing it for five years in succession is.

The year 2011 was the team's 47th display season and as Ben put it, 'There is only so much you can do as most of it has already been done before. A new manoeuvre is difficult to design and requires a lot of work to prefect, so it tends to be a case of re-introducing a previous formation and modifying it with a slightly different manoeuvre.' For example, the Whirlwind was previously used as a seven-ship manoeuvre in 2010 but was modified as a nine-ship manoeuvre in the 24-minute 2011 programme. Also new for 2011 was the rear crowd entry with the outside two aircraft rolling after they passed overhead.

It was little surprise that Sqn Ldr Jim Turner was appointed to lead the team in 2012. He had already served with the Red Arrows for three years, from 2005 to 2007, in a variety of positions. At the end of his tour, he was seconded to the Royal Saudi Air Force and become Team Adviser to the Saudi Hawks, helping that team develop into the dynamic six-ship Hawk display team that appeared alongside the Red Arrows at the 2011 Royal International Air Tattoo at Fairford. Jim had plans to develop the shape and complexity of some of the manoeuvres for 2012 but, following the unfortunate ejector seat incident that led to the death of Red 5, Flt Lt Sean Cunningham, only weeks into the training schedule, and a five-week lay-off as a result

The team at the top of the Swan Loop, at the Cromer Carnival in August 2011. As the formation moves up to the top of the loop, the inside pair of aircraft stop smoking and the team moves into Typhoon as it transitions over the top for the upcoming Typhoon Twist. *(Keith Wilson)*

For the Rolling and Flat Display, the Swan Loop becomes the sweeping Swan Reversal, as seen at the Lowestoft seafront display on 12 August 2011. *(Keith Wilson)*

Coming down from the Swan Loop, the team has cleverly moved into the Typhoon Twist. The black lead aircraft indicates the venue as the Cromer Carnival in August 2011. *(Keith Wilson)*

of the initial enquiry and currency training, it was back to the drawing board. The programme had to be changed in light of the reduced training programme available, to something that was both realistic and achievable, giving the shortened time scales. Consequently, four or five new or modified manoeuvres were removed or simplified. The planned show for 2012 consists of a nine-ship first half and a split second half without any gaps, lasting about 20 minutes – displaying aesthetically pleasing shapes.

The author asked Jim Turner which manoeuvres he thought would be difficult: 'The Swan manoeuvre in the first half – rolling it would take forever to practise but looping the shape will be ok, and the nine-ship Quarter Clover with a twist into a bend is going to be tough too. Rollbacks for the Enid are challenging for both accuracy and looking symmetrical. For the Synchro Pair, the inverted flying is always difficult while the timing for Red 9 coming back from Goose to crowd-centre will take some practice to get it just right.'

Whichever show you watch, be it the Full, Rolling or Flat display, you will see aerobatic display flying at its very best. After all, the Red Arrows are probably the world's leading jet formation display team.

For the Rolling or Flat Display, Typhoon Twist becomes the Typhoon Bend and is flown as a relatively flat manoeuvre in front of the crowd line. *(Keith Wilson)*

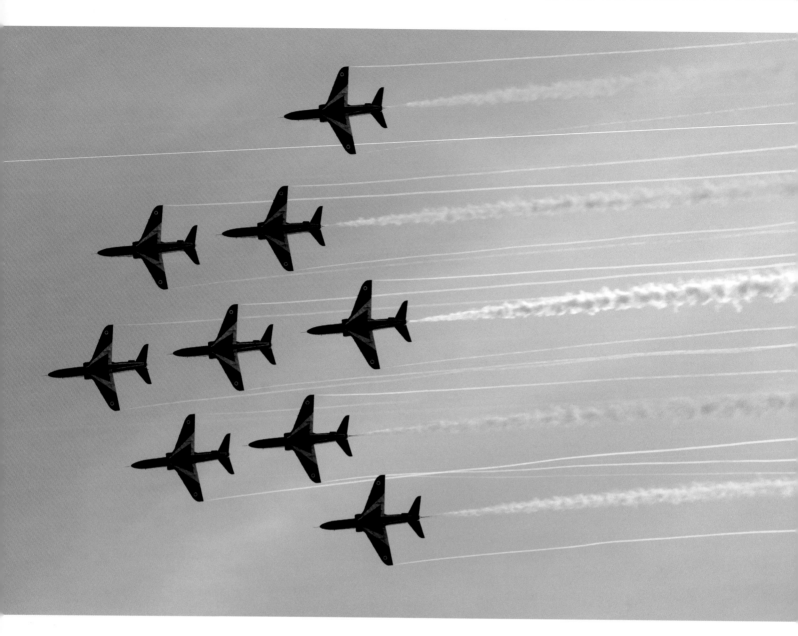

The Apollo Twister, a manoeuvre flown in both the Full and Rolling Display programme for 2011. For the Flat Display, this manoeuvre becomes a flat Apollo Reversal. Operating relatively close to the water, the team has flown through moist air and the wingtip vortices are evidence of that at Eastbourne's Airbourne 2011 seafront event. *(Keith Wilson)*

The Flanker formation, a relatively difficult team manoeuvre, was flown during all three display variations in 2011 and is photographed at the RIAT on 17 July 2011. *(Keith Wilson)*

From the Apollo formation, Red 4 and 5 roll as the team moves to Eagle formation. This spectacular view was obtained by being directly underneath the flight line of the display, permitting a head-on view – not something usually available to airshow visitors with today's safety-conscious procedures.
(EJ van Koningsveld)

From Flanker, the team moves through Eagle to Diamond Bend, as shown during the Rolling Display at Lowestoft in August 2011.
(Keith Wilson)

A difficult manoeuvre for the team to perfect is the Whirlwind, flown in Loose Diamond formation during both Full and Flat Displays. Getting the timing and rate of roll to perfection is tough. *(Oliver Wilson)*

An unusual and privileged view of the Eagle formation, as seen from above, during practice over Akrotiri, Cyprus, on 14 April 2011. The image was taken from Red 10, flown by Sqn Ldr Graeme Bagnall. *(EJ van Koningsveld)*

The Blackbird, a difficult nine-ship rolling manoeuvre that featured in the team's 2010 display sequence but was not repeated in 2011. *(EJ van Koningsveld)*

Flying a team with aircraft in both line-astern and line-abreast simultaneously is hard work, but the Tango formation featured in the 2010 display looks good. *(EJ van Koningsveld)*

Another difficult manoeuvre that features line-abreast formation is the Phoenix. This was flown during both the 2010 and 2011 display sequence. *(EJ van Koningsveld)*

Λ Similar to both Big Nine and Big Vixen, the Chevron formation was used in 2010. *(EJ van Koningsveld)*

➤ A most unusual and difficult formation to fly is the Kite, used in 2006 but not repeated since. It bears a similarity with the seven-ship Vixen formation, Reds 8 and 9 completing the tail of the Kite. *(EJ van Koningsveld)*

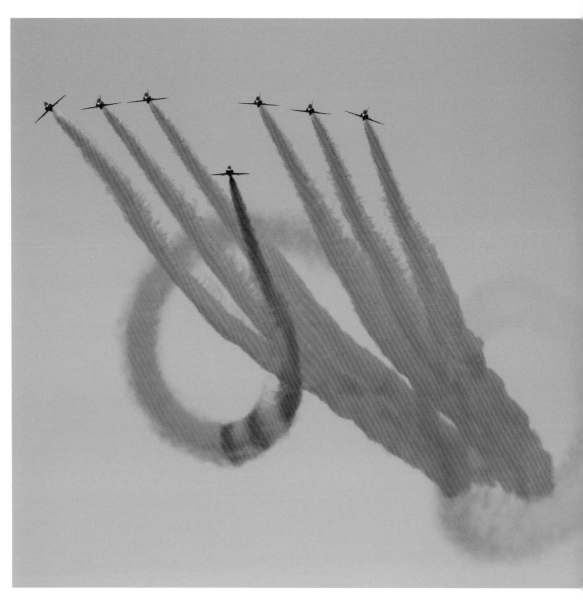

◄ The Red Arrows' display is usually split into two halves; the first half features a range of sweeping and graceful nine-ship manoeuvres, while the second half tends to feature smaller formations of more dynamic manoeuvres. There comes a point in the programme when the full nine-ship needs to split into the five-ship Enid and four-ship Gypo sections. In the full programme of 2011, the Palm Split was cleverly used to get Reds 8 and 9 away from the main formation, as seen at the Cromer Carnival in August 2011.
(Keith Wilson)

Λ The spectacular seven-ship Infinity Break was used in the 2010 programme and featured Red 1 rolling around the remaining six aircraft while trailing red smoke, just before all seven aircraft broke in all directions.
(EJ van Koningsveld)

➢ The ideal location to view the dynamic and spectacular Gypo Break is at 90° to the centre of the crowd line. Reds 8 and 9 barrel-roll around Reds 6 and 7 who spot-roll before the opposition break.
(EJ van Koningsveld)

◄ The first of four dynamic views of the Gypo Break sequence, with Reds 6, 7, 8 and 9 appearing to be heading for each other. *(EJ van Koningsveld)*

⩔ The second of four dynamic views of the Gypo Break sequence. *(EJ van Koningsveld)*

➤ The third of four dynamic views of the Gypo Break sequence. *(EJ van Koningsveld)*

⋎ The fourth and final shot of the Gypo Break sequence, with Reds 6, 7, 8 and 9 having successfully managed to avoid striking one another. *(Jose van Koningsveld)*

◄ The Vertical Break in
the 2011 Full Display
involved the five-ship Enid
section looping, followed
by a fan split away from
the crowd, as seen at
Eastbourne's Airbourne
2011 seafront show.
(Keith Wilson)

The Cyclone, another manoeuvre involving the Synchro Pair in opposition using their blue and red smoke to good effect, flying low over the water at Eastbourne in August 2011. (Keith Wilson)

The Vixen Break, a spectacular manoeuvre at the end of the Rolling Display flown at Lowestoft in August 2011. The seven-ship formation uses an alternating white-red-white-blue smoke pattern, along with an on-crowd fan split, to very good effect. (Oliver Wilson)

◄ A relatively simple looking manoeuvre, but difficult to fly neatly, is the five-ship line-astern pass flown by the Enid section. *(EJ van Koningsveld)*

A The Corkscrew is another manoeuvre that proved popular during both 2010 and 2011. Reds 6 and 7 fly inverted along the crowd line, trailing white smoke, while Reds 8 and 9 roll around them with red and blue smoke trailing. *(EJ van Koningsveld)*

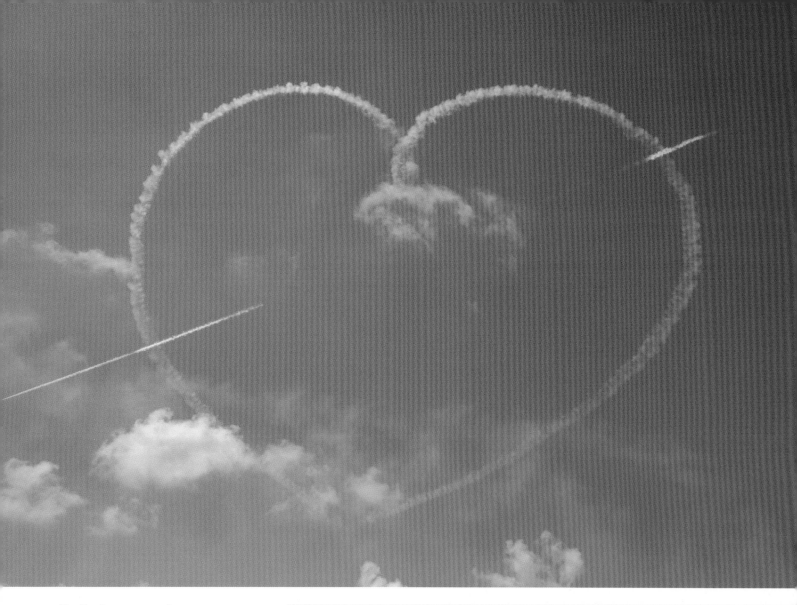

The Heart manoeuvre was only flown during the Full Display routines in both 2010 and 2011 and usually brought noisy 'oohs' and 'aahs' from the watching crowd. The main body of the heart was flown by the Synchro Pair (Reds 6 and 7), while the spear was flown by Red 9. In 2010, the team used white smoke for the manoeuvre but changed this to red smoke in 2011, although it was not always as prominent as it might have been, particularly on windy days. *(EJ van Koningsveld)*

➤ At the end of the display, and assuming they are landing back at the event, the team enters along the runway in a nine-ship Run and Break before they individually break-right away from the main formation, in team order, then fly downwind in trail to land. Reds 1, 2 and 3 had already broken from the formation during an ISP at Scampton in August 2011. *(Keith Wilson)*

➤ Occasionally, rather than finish the display with a classic Run and Break, the team ends with the Spag Break. This involves all nine aircraft looping before heading earthwards and breaking in all directions; then joining downwind to land in turn. This Spag Break was photographed during a display practice at Akrotiri in 2011, from chase plane Red 10 flown by Sqn Ldr Graeme Bagnall. *(EJ van Koningsveld)*

Working Up
Practice makes Perfect

When the Red Arrows returned to Scampton on 27 September 2011, after having flown with the Patrouille de France at their home base at Salon in the South of France, they had completed 70 displays during the 2011 season. Despite being a difficult season, the event was marked with the traditional champagne.

It had been a traumatic year for the team, marred by the fatal accident of Flt Lt Jon Egging and the six eight-ship displays flown thereafter as a consequence of the tragic loss. In October, the pilots headed off to complete the Jon Egging Coast to Coast Challenge, a 400 miles in 4 days cycle ride undertaken with members of the Battle of Britain Memorial Flight (BBMF) to raise money for the various charities supported by both teams. At the end of the event, three pilots – Sqn Ldr Ben Murphy, Flt Lt David Montenegro and Flt Lt Zane Sennett – left the team to take up new roles.

While the 2011 team members were cycling from St David's Head to Lowestoft, the new members gathered at Scampton to begin training. Led by a new team leader for 2012, Sqn Ldr Jim Turner (Red 1), the Reds also welcomed Flt Lt Martin Pert (Red 2), Flt Lt Mike Child (Red 3) and Flt Lt James McMillan (Red 4) into their ranks and it wasn't long before the new boys were occupying the hot seats in the Hawk jets.

➤ **The Red Arrows during an Apollo ¼ Clover manoeuvre over RAF Scampton in August 2007. The photograph was taken with a 10mm fisheye lens from cameraship XX242 with Red 11, Wg Cdr David Middleton, at the controls.**
(EJ van Koningsveld)

Training programme

In the working-up process for the annual award of the Public Display Authority (PDA), a carefully planned training programme is undertaken, with weather and maintenance issues usually providing the biggest adversaries. The PDA is ultimately awarded by the Air Officer Commanding No 22 (Training) Group. It recognises the team's level of display safety and professionalism, and must be awarded before they can perform in front of the public. With the first public display planned for the beginning of June 2012, there is a great deal to be achieved if the first scheduled performance is to be met.

Once training begins in September, all members of the squadron revert to wearing green flying suits and overalls. The programme begins with small formations of three or four aircraft as the new pilots learn flying references and formation shapes. Each pilot flies three times a day, five days a week; progress is rapid and improvement often significant.

Sqn Ldr Ben Murphy led the working-up programmes for the 2010 and 2011 seasons. He says, 'All positions are new so we are effectively working from scratch. We go back to basics and adopt a building-block approach.' Each year the team has three new members, who occupy Red 2 through to Red 4 and initial formation training is developed around these aircraft. Red 5 – usually a more experienced member of the team who earns the nickname 'Uncle Enid' – joins the formation as it increases to a five-ship.

⋀ **Sqn Ldr Jim Turner (Red 1) leads the pre-flight briefing at Scampton before a four-ship training flight in October 2011. Looking on are Flt Lt Martin Pert (Red 2), Flt Lt Mike Child (Red 3) and Flt Lt James McMillan (Red 4).** *(Keith Wilson)*

➤ **Reds 1, 2, 3 and 4 departing from Scampton's main runway on a four-ship training sortie in October 2011.** *(Keith Wilson)*

➤ With four new team members for the 2012 display season, including the team leader, joining at the end of September 2011, every opportunity is taken to practise the various manoeuvres. The process begins with small formations of three or four aircraft with three training slots a day flown, five days a week. *(Keith Wilson)*

⌄ Every sortie flown by the Red Arrows – whether for training or a full air-show display – has to be recorded on video. After the pilots have landed, the sortie is debriefed in minute detail using the video footage. Cpl Graham Taylor, one of the team photographers, is suitably protected from the cold autumn weather during a Red Arrows' training sortie at Scampton in October 2011. *(Keith Wilson)*

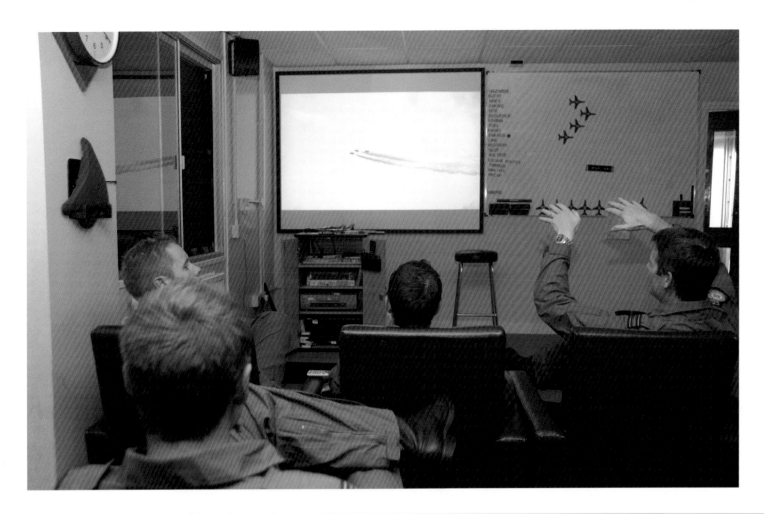

△ Sqn Ldr Jim Turner (Red 1) leads the post-flight debriefing with Reds 2, 3 and 4 after a training flight at Scampton in October 2011. The video of the flight can be seen on the screen in front of them. The team's standards are incredibly high and something is learned from every flight. *(Keith Wilson)*

◁ The four new Red Arrows' team members for the 2012 display season were practising formation line-astern flying at Scampton in early October 2011 – at this early stage not always showing the tightest of formation flying. *(Keith Wilson)*

➤ Line-astern is not an easy formation to fly and later in the same sortie, the improvements were obvious. *(Keith Wilson)*

Formation references are made from Red 1 at all times, so as the formation increases in size from four, to five, and on to six and seven, all are flown with the team leader at the front.

'The winter training programme is a great opportunity to build trust among the team,' says Murphy, 'although, along with the daily flying training, it is also a busy period for the team with numerous corporate and PR activities to accommodate.'

Meanwhile, the Synchro Pair, Reds 6 and 7, are working up their own formation training, initially flying as singletons in order to obtain ground and display timing references, before taking to the air together. Accurate timing runs for the team leader and the Synchro leader are imperative to ensure that the overall programme fits together nicely. Red 6 as Synchro Leader will have flown as Red 7, Synchro 2, the previous year.

Every sortie is thoroughly briefed before it is flown and recorded on video from the ground by a member of the team's photographic section. Shortly after the team has landed the evidence is delivered to the briefing room and the sortie is thoroughly debriefed in minute detail. Using 16x zoom magnification video equipment, the footage clearly shows errors of just 1–2ft (0.3–0.6m), such is the demand for accurate flying among the team. Slowly and safely, the overall display sequence is developed.

Normally, the plan is to get seven aircraft in formation by November and the first nine-ship at the beginning of March, while the team still training in the UK. For the 2011 display season, delays due to adverse weather had prevented the nine-ship formation taking to the skies, so this landmark formation wasn't flown until the team arrived in Cyprus for 'Exercise Springhawk' in March 2011.

➤ Another view from Red 6, flown by Flt Lt SD Stephens, photographed going over the top of a loop near Scampton during an ISP in August 2006. (EJ van Koningsveld)

⋎ The Big Vixen Roll above Scampton in August 2007, taken using a 10mm fisheye lens. The cameraship – Red 11 – is, on this occasion, flown by Wg Cdr David Middleton. (EJ van Koningsveld)

⋀ **Enjoying the view from Red 11. The team in formation over the Alps, between Clermont-Ferrand, France, and Rivolto, Italy – home of the Frecce Tricolori – while en route to Akrotiri, Cyprus, 18 March 2011. The shot was taken from XX284, flown by CFS pilot Flt Lt 'Shep' Sheppard.** *(Squadron Leader Ross Priday)*

◁ **Spectacular view of the Red Arrows in a Diamond Loop before entering the Spag Break above Scampton in August 2007. Once again, the cameraship was Red 11, flown by Wg Cdr David Middleton.** *(EJ van Koningsveld)*

➢ **Gypo formation descending from altitude for a refuelling stop at Rivolto, while en route to Akrotiri, 18 March 2011. The shot was taken from Red 11, XX284, flown by CFS pilot Flt Lt 'Shep' Sheppard.** *(Sqn Ldr Ross Priday)*

Triumph and tragedy

During the autumn of 2011, the Lincolnshire weather was kind to the team and progress among the new members was impressive. For the first two weeks, all new team members spent time flying with the team leader in the back seat – to assess and refine their style of flying and throttle movement. Once this initial training had been concluded, the four-ship developed quickly and assisted by either Sqn Ldr Graeme Bagnall or Sqn Ldr Martin Higgins (Red 10) occupying the Red 5 position, five-ship formations were undertaken relatively early on in the programme. Airframes were made available by the hard-working engineering team and progress continued at a pace.

Sadly, the tragic loss of Flt Lt Sean Cunningham (Red 5) on the morning of 8 November 2011, and the precautionary grounding of all Royal Air Force aircraft fitted with the Mk 10 ejector seat, undid the early progress and pushed the training programme behind schedule.

On 9 December 2011, the MoD announced that sufficient technical and safety advice had been obtained from the service inquiry to release all Hawk T1 aircraft, including those of the Red Arrows, back into service. Following a short period of staff continuation training, the team recommenced their work-up a week later. However, Christmas was on the horizon, when they take a three-week break from flying to recharge their personal batteries and the Scampton base closes.

At the beginning of 2012, working up continued in earnest with each pilot flying three training trips a day, five days a week – the weather and the availability of serviceable airframes being the usual limitations. Snow prevented training on a number of days in January and February when the runway could not be cleared. Unlike frontline RAF Stations, Scampton as a training base does not possess full snow-clearing capabilities. If snow was to become a longer-term problem, there is a contingency plan to move training down to the relatively warmer climes of Newquay International Airport, formerly RAF St Mawgan in Cornwall, which historically has less snow than Lincolnshire and possesses the required clearing equipment. However, while training sorties would increase, the logistical issues associated with moving large parts of the squadron during the busiest maintenance period would have serious consequences. Expected snowfalls in Lincolnshire would have to be significant before the plan was activated. In addition, Newquay is now a civilian airport, and this would add a further complexity to the training planning and execution and involve fitting practice slots among arriving and departing commercial flights.

◁ **The team practising over Akrotiri on 6 May 2009 – going over the Diamond Loop before entering the Spag Break. Cameraship was Red 10, XX292, flown by Sqn Ldr Graeme Bagnall.** *(EJ van Koningsveld)*

▷ **Viewed from the ground, an early morning shot of the team in Eagle formation during a practice session at Akrotiri, 19 May 2010.** *(EJ van Koningsveld)*

The setbacks suffered by the team towards the end of 2011 meant that the planned display programme for 2012 has been cleverly amended in an attempt to reduce training demands. Four or five new manoeuvres have been removed or adjusted. The nine-ship first-half and split second-half programme will now be exactly 20 minutes with no gaps in the second half. It will consist of aesthetically pleasing, entertaining shapes and, more importantly, will be achievable within the time remaining.

Sqn Ldr Turner says, 'Flying in the early part of 2012 has progressed well with the five-ship being seen together regularly. Effort is being concentrated on the shape changes as well as the cadence of the radio calls, which can assist with the formation and manoeuvre changes. Inputs on flying controls for all positions need refinement and all team members are getting used to being in exactly the right place. The video identifies any small errors (of just a few feet) and we can then correct and eliminate them.'

Λ The team in Big Battle formation just before turning in for the break to land. This shot was taken from Red 9, flown by Flt Lt SP Rea, over Akrotiri, 12 May 2010. *(EJ van Koningsveld)*

⊰ Red 9, XX306, flown by Flt Lt AR Keith, rolls neatly into position to take its place for the next formation. The photograph was taken from Red 6, XX260, flown by Flt Lt P O'Grady, 14 May 2010. *(EJ van Koningsveld)*

⋎ Up nice and close behind the team leader, Sqn Ldr Ben Murphy, during a team formation loop over Akrotiri, 14 May 2010. The photograph was taken from Red 6, flown by Flt Lt P O'Grady. *(EJ van Koningsveld)*

Synchro Pair shape up

Progress with the Synchro Pair's training continues. Initially, the Synchro leader flies as a singleton to perfect the patterns and all-important radio calls. Meanwhile, Synchro 2 learns everything from scratch – initially as a singleton – working down from 1,500ft (457m) to the regularly display height. Once both are happy they commence training on the opposition breaking manoeuvres. Minimum display separation for these manoeuvres is 100ft (30m), although they start with a 200ft (60m) separation – coincidentally, the width of Scampton's main runway. They also practise inverted flying as a pair until perfected.

The Synchro leader for 2012 is Flt Lt Ben Plank (Red 6) who is in his third year with the team. Ben flew as Red 2 in 2010 and as Synchro 2 during 2011. The Synchro 2 slot for the 2012 season has been passed to Flt Lt Chris Lyndon-Smith (Red 7) who flew as Red 2 in 2011.

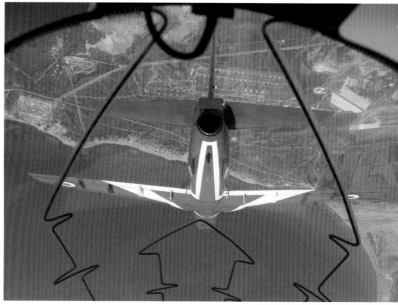

⋀ The team moves into Diamond Formation during a vertical climb over Akrotiri, 14 May 2010. The photograph was taken from Red 6, flown by Flt Lt P O'Grady. *(EJ van Koningsveld)*

➢ The team going over the top of a Phoenix Loop, beautifully framed by the Akrotiri coastline. Photographed from Red 8, flown by Sqn Ldr G Duff, 19 May 2010. *(EJ van Koningsveld)*

⋀ Another practice over Akrotiri, this time on 13 May 2010. The shot was taken from Red 9, flown by Flt Lt SP Rea, as the team turns in for the Gypo Break. *(EJ van Koningsveld)*

➢ The team in Phoenix formation over the Mediterranean while being 'chased' by Red 10, XX177, flown by Sqn Ldr Graeme Bagnall, 20 May 2010. *(EJ van Koningsveld)*

The team changing formation at the top of a loop during practice. Photographed from Red 9, flown by Flt Lt SP Rea, 13 May 2010.
(EJ van Koningsveld)

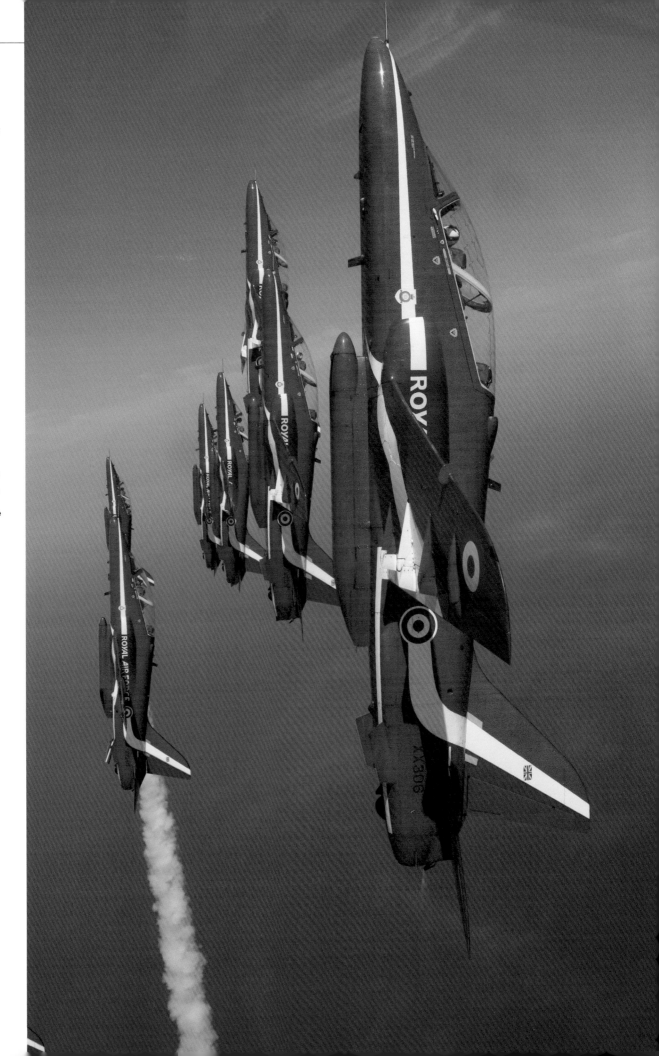

➤ Seven of the remaining eight aircraft in the formation are visible in this beautiful study of the team as they climb vertically in Phoenix. The tail of Red 8 can just be seen in the bottom left and may be slightly out of position. The picture was taken from Red 9, flown by Flt Lt SP Rea, 13 May 2010.
(EJ van Koningsveld)

◄ Another spectacular image of the team in Diamond, as they go over the top of the loop before entering the Spag Break during a practice on 20 May 2010. The image was taken from Red 10, flown by Sqn Ldr Graeme Bagnall.
(EJ van Koningsveld)

Reds 8 and 9

For Reds 8 and 9, practice is not quite so straightforward, although both are experienced members of the team. Red 8 is Flt Lt Dave Davies who is in his fourth year, having occupied the Red 4 (twice) and Red 8 slots. The Red 9 slot for 2012 will be taken by Flt Lt Kirsty Stewart who is in her third year with the team. Kirsty is the first female member of the Red Arrows and in 2012 will be undertaking the important Executive Officer role as part of Red 9's duties.

Reds 8 and 9 often fly together with Reds 1 to 5 ('Enid') to ensure the first half of the programme is formulated, but they are also required to practise with the Synchro Pair to ensure that the Gypo four-ship section of the programme, flown during the second half of the routine, is similarly perfected.

Operation Springhawk

By the time the team leave for Exercise Springhawk in Cyprus on 15 March 2012, they will be well behind with the training programme for the 2012 display season and the issue of the all-important PDA. The team has not been helped by the low number of airframes available to it – especially those equipped with the all-important smoke-making equipment. Only the team leader is permitted to fly without the smoke-generating equipment as the smoke is a crucial formation aid, especially during the joining-up phases, and is used extensively during the second half of the display.

Getting the team out to Cyprus, along with all its equipment, is a difficult logistical exercise. It requires airlift capabilities from DSCOM

The Vixen Break, the final manoeuvre of the 2011 season, is practised at Akrotiri on 12 April. *(EJ van Koningsveld)*

The very best place to view the Gypo Break is at 90° from show centre. Although not quite the perfect position, this is a great shot of the spectacular manoeuvre being practised on 13 April 2011. *(EJ van Koningsveld)*

The view at the top of a loop from Red 5, flown by Flt Lt Kirsty Stewart, on 12 April 2011. The Akrotiri runway is visible in the bottom of the image. (EJ. van Koningsveld)

(the RAF's Defence Support Chain – Operations and Movements), which would normally provide an RAF Hercules C4. If one is not available, due to operational commitments elsewhere across the globe, the team makes its request to NATO's MCCE (Movement Co-ordination Centre Europe), headquartered in Eindhoven. In the past, this has meant being supported on their travels by a pair of German Air Force C160s or a Hercules aircraft from the Danish, Dutch or Norwegian Air Forces. Currently, the team is expecting a single RAF Hercules to carry its equipment and engineers across to Akrotiri in March 2012.

At the time of writing, the team will fly to Akrotiri with only 7 or possibly 8 Hawk jets; normally, there would be 11 or 12. Three or four additional Hawks are expected to be delivered during the exercise, eventually allowing the team to operate with a full complement. Then members can enjoy the benefits of the Mediterranean weather and the relatively clear air space that Akrotiri has to offer in order to practise their routine two or three times a day against some wonderful coastal landmarks.

Normally, the team flies its first nine-ship formation at the beginning of March, before departing for Cyprus. In 2012, for numerous reasons, this will not be possible and it is expected that the first nine-ship will be flown while at Akrotiri. Jim Turner anticipates that by then 'they will be at a 75% solution stage' and will need the 'next two months to practise up to a 95% solution stage by tightening timings and refining the shapes'.

Normally, the PDA is issued at the end of Exercise Springhawk, but this year it is possible that the team will return home in their green flying suits. Once back in the UK, and with further opportunities to practise and refine the display routine, it is expected that the AOC will make an assessment of their safety and professionalism and if satisfied, will award Public Display Authority. Only then will the team members be allowed to wear their prestigious red flying suits for the first time.

Training for the 2012 season has been, and will continue to be, tough. Once the PDA has been issued, the hard work continues for the pilots and support personnel as they enter the display season.

The team in Phoenix formation over the Mediterranean on 15 April 2011, photographed from 'chase' Red 10, flown by Sqn Ldr Graeme Bagnall. Note the position of the pilots' heads while maintaining station on the leader during this difficult formation manoeuvre. (EJ van Koningsveld)

➤ Practice makes perfect! The perfect Diamond formation continues right above the runway at Akrotiri on 15 April 2011, just before the team comes over the top of the loop and enters the Spag Break. Photographed from Red 10, XX284, flown by Sqn Ldr Graeme Bagnall. *(EJ van Koningsveld)*

➤ Another spectacular fisheye-lens shot as the team enters the Vertical Break high over the Mediterranean. Perfect timing with the chase aircraft – Red 10, flown by Sqn Ldr Graeme Bagnall – and the main formation was crucial to obtain this shot. *(EJ van Koningsveld)*

➤ The Eagle formation shot from above the formation over the Mediterranean, near RAF Akrotiri, 14 April 2011. Once again the photograph was shot from Red 10, flown by Sqn Ldr Graeme Bagnall. This was a particularly difficult image to obtain as the photographer was unable to look through the camera viewfinder; instead, he had to guess where to aim the camera over his shoulder. *(EJ van Koningsveld)*

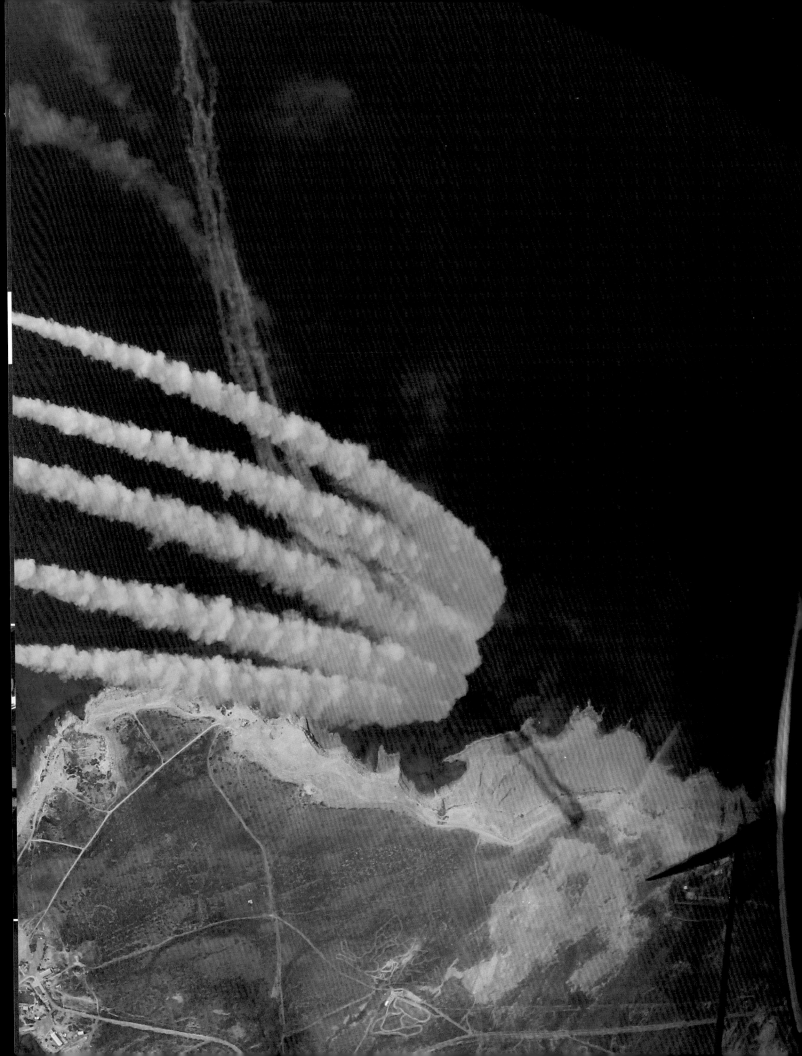

The Red Arrows have just 9 pilots, 12 aircraft and around 80 engineers to keep them flying and complete the season's displays – which in 2011 amounted to 70 shows in 8 countries. While the ratio of engineers to pilots and aircraft may, at first sight, seem a little high, it is in fact the lowest of any Royal Air Force fast jet squadron. It emphasises the efficiency and teamwork that exists on this unique squadron – with the key word being 'teamwork'.

➢ **Hawk T1 XX260 undergoing maintenance at RAF Scampton in July 2011. The aircraft is raised up on jacks in preparation for an undercarriage sequence check.** *(Keith Wilson)*

The role of the Senior Engineering Officer

The role of the Senior Engineering Officer

Heading the engineering team at RAF Scampton is the Senior Engineering Officer (SEngO), Sqn Ldr Ross Priday. Ross joined the RAF in 1990 as an aircraft engineer and was commissioned as an officer in 2001, reaching the rank of Squadron Leader in 2007. He has held a variety of key engineering posts in the RAF, with previous experience on both the Typhoon and Tornado aircraft, and he also served on Operation Telic with the Nimrod MR2 force in 2003.

Ross has responsibility for all engineering and logistical matters for the team, but he sees his role as strategic – especially with the maintenance operations of the Red Arrows' fleet of Hawk jets. He is home-base oriented and leaves the day-to-day Circus business in the capable hands of his Junior Engineering Officer (JEngO), Flt Lt Adam Littler, who leads the famous blue-overalls all over the UK and Europe, with occasional trips further afield.

The strategic responsibility sees Ross concerned about the long-term sustainability of the team – both in terms of aircraft and their ongoing maintenance – and he plans to replace most of the team's tools and tooling in the next two years, as well as procuring more rugged toolkits for overseas deployments.

There is the small matter of overhauling all the Hawk aircraft during the early winter period. Each aircraft takes between 4 and 16 weeks to complete and the work runs to a very tight schedule to ensure that all are ready on time, while ensuring that a sufficient number of airframes are available to the team during its winter work-up programme. All of this maintenance happens concurrently with the winter flying training programme to ensure that not just the aircrew but also the aircraft are ready for the next display season.

⚊ The Circus engineering team preparing for an In Season Practice (ISP) and deployment to Bournemouth, 5 August 2011. The meeting is being conducted by Circus leader Sergeant Matt Lord (left) with SEngO Flt Lt Adam Littler (red suit) and the remaining Circus members – SAC Geraldine Beaton, Cpl Dave Howard, Cpl Scott Aston, Cpl Jamie Hatcher, SAC Simon Watkins, SAC Joe Sproat, Cpl Chris Moss and Cpl Kev Smith – looking on. *(Keith Wilson)*

Ross is also co-ordinating a Hawk Replacement Programme (HRP) which will see nine 'new' aircraft delivered to the team during the next three years. The first, XX319, arrived at Scampton in August 2011 ready for the 2012 season. Six jets have been with the Reds since 1979, while the youngest aircraft on the team was delivered to the RAF in 1980. Many, if not all, have high flying hours and, more importantly, high fatigue index (FI). This often makes the air-show planning a bit of a juggling act as only certain aircraft are allowed to be used by the Synchro Pair because the stresses on these aircraft are significantly higher than on the others.

Close cooperation with BAe Systems has seen the permitted FI level increase from a previous ceiling of 150 up to 165. This has allowed some of the team aircraft merely to continue in service for another couple of seasons at best, but it has not actually fixed the problem. Most aircraft use between one and two units of FI per month, with between six and seven being used in an average year. Currently, RAFAT replacement Hawks are stored at RAF Shawbury – many with both low flying hours and FI – and these will be overhauled as part of the programme and will join the team as they become ready.

Then there is the question of Adour engines. The Red Arrows' aircraft have a modified powerplant (Mk 102) to ensure a quicker throttle response time compared with the standard training Hawk airframes. Ross has one more engine than aircraft in his inventory –

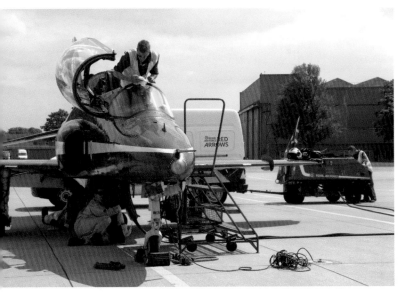

◁ Viewed through the open canopy of another team Hawk, XX308 is refuelled by Circus 3 (Cpl Dave Howard) assisted by Sgt Kieran Lambe, a member of the team's Mechanical Transport (MT) section. _(Keith Wilson)_

∨ While diesel is loaded into the centreline smoke pod by a member of the MT section at Scampton, SAC Joe Sproat (Circus 9) cleans the undersides of his aircraft (Red 9) in preparation for the next display. _(Keith Wilson)_

∧ The flight line is a hive of activity immediately after the team have landed. All aircraft have to be refuelled, the dye tanks replenished and canopies cleaned before the next display slot – normally about 90 minutes later. Here the Dye Team is at work, while Cpl Jamie Hatcher (Circus 6) cleans the canopy of Red 6. _(Keith Wilson)_

◁ A Circus team member monitors the fuel uptake to ensure the correct quantity is loaded for the next flight by visually checking the fuel gauge in the front cockpit; SAC Mark Jones, a member of the team's MT section, looks after the tanker. _(Keith Wilson)_

SAC's Glynn West and Jason Stanway of the Dye Team in action. Special protective goggles and suits are worn by the team as the dye can cause permanent marking on clothes. The engineer places his ear against the front of the smoke pod to ensure that the dye is entering correctly, while the engineer at the rear of the pod is listening to hear when the pod is full. *(Keith Wilson)*

Suitably attired, Dye Team member SAC Jason Stanway has an ear to the centreline smoke pod. It is important to stop the flow of dye just before any surplus is pumped into the overflow drum. Some does occasionally get spilt and decorates the ramp at Scampton. *(Keith Wilson)*

Controlling the flow and monitoring the dye uptake is Dye Team leader Cpl Rhys Martin on the Scampton ramp on 3 July 2011. *(Keith Wilson)*

not exactly a luxurious situation. The engine also has fatigue life issues and the Module 1 Change has become more regular than expected, meaning more engine removals and overhauls for the hard-working engineers in the hangar at Scampton.

Ross heads a strong, closely-knit team where he feels the 'level of trust is amazing' and where the team ethos is one of 'trust and teamwork'. Aside from the JEngO, there is the Flight Sergeant Engineering – who Ross describes as the team 'Rottweiler' – responsible for manning and manpower issues as well as the all-important discipline. Currently, the role is filled by Flt Sgt Steve Cox, who has been in the post for three-and-a-half years of a five-year tour and who recently received an AOC Commendation in the 2011 New Year's Honours List.

The Circus Leader, a role which Ross describes as 'The Provider', is filled by an experienced Sergeant on an annual change basis. In 2011, it was undertaken by Matt Lord, a mechanical technician who also operated as Circus 8.

Other critical roles include the Dye Team Leader, a Road Rectifications Controller, a Road Doc's Controller, Planning, MT and the Quest Leader – heading an engineering support team. With only 80 engineers, Ross insists that 'each and every one of them is crucial to the overall success of the team'.

⋀ Replenishing the oxygen system on Red 6 at Scampton in July 2011 is Cpl Jamie Hatcher (Circus 6). *(Keith Wilson)*

⋁ Good use is made of display boards such as these by members of the Red Arrows maintenance team at RAF Scampton. On this board, located in the main engineering room, the status of each aircraft is clearly visible: green tags indicate 'available', red tags indicate 'unavailable'. *(Keith Wilson)*

➤ When a problem was discovered with the port main wheel assembly on XX264, Sgt Mark Bennett and SAC Mark Cummings were sent to fit a new one. With the main gear leg jacked-up and a specialist tool kit available for the task (foreground), the wheel assembly is replaced in no time. *(Keith Wilson)*

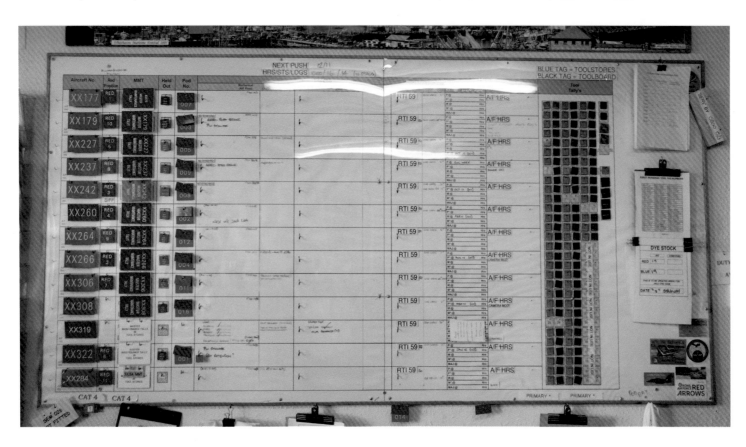

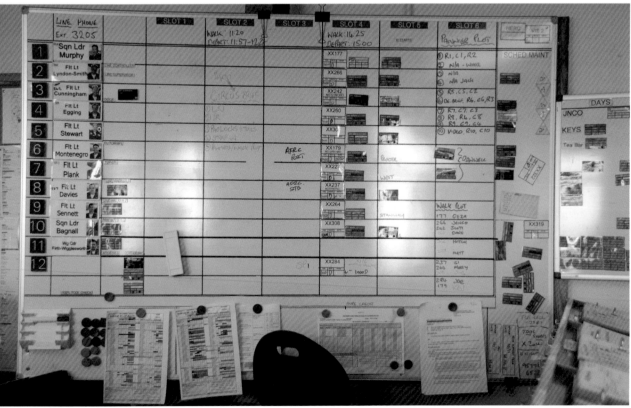

A A busy ramp scene at Scampton, 5 August 2011. Cpl Dave Howard (Circus 3) drags the refuelling hose towards Red 3 while other engineers are busy with their own aircraft. *(Keith Wilson)*

◄ Another display board in the engineering room at Scampton shows which aircraft have been allocated to which team member for the push to Bournemouth on 5 August 2011. It also indicates the required fuel loading to each aircraft as well as the luggage panniers being used for the transit. *(Keith Wilson)*

While Ross is normally deskbound at Scampton, he regularly joins the team as Circus 11 when all 11 aircraft are involved in a push – for example, on Exercise Springhawk, the team's winter training programme usually held at Akrotiri, Cyprus. Ross normally flies in the back of Red 11, with Wg Cdr David Firth-Wigglesworth, the team's Senior Flying Supervisor and Officer Commanding Operations Wing at RAF Scampton. The pair are affectionately known as the 'vintage pair' or 'Saga flight' when they fly together.

During the air-show season, Ross's engineering role is to ensure that the team have ten good aircraft at all times. Although the standard fleet is 13 aircraft, at the time of writing, the team had only nine red and a single black Hawk loaned from RAF Valley on strength; this is often difficult, to say the least. The ethos is to ensure that a spare aircraft is available at all times, just in case of a last-minute hitch with another airframe. For an 11-aircraft push, that effectively means that 12 aircraft must be available – no mean feat! For the more normal 10-aircraft airshow requirement (nine display aircraft plus the Team Manager/Commentator's aircraft, which also acts as a spare), that still means getting 11 aircraft up and ready to go. Consequently, members of the engineering team do not work in a 9-to-5, five-days-a-week job. Thankfully, they are a dedicated bunch, working weekends and long hours to get the job done.

⊼ **Final preparation for the push to Bournemouth on 5 August 2011. The entire Circus team are on the ramp making last-minute preparations to their aircraft. Note that all aircraft remain earthed to the ground at all times while parked on the ramp.** *(Keith Wilson)*

➤ **While Cpl Lee Proctor fills the centreline dye pod, SAC Simon Watkins (Circus 7) is inspecting the engine inlet. Every nook and cranny on every aircraft is inspected by the Circus team before each flight.** *(Keith Wilson)*

For two weeks in July, the team takes a break from display flying to allow the engineers a chance to work on the aircraft. Here, in the Red Arrows' hangar at Scampton in July 2011, all the aircraft are present for maintenance. *(Keith Wilson)*

XX308 has the benefit of three engineers – SAC Ben Laiking, Cpl Dale Spridgens and SAC Glen Jones – working on the Adour engine at Scampton on 28 July 2011. It is not easy to work on the engine from below so all available assets are utilised to make the task a little more comfortable. *(Keith Wilson)*

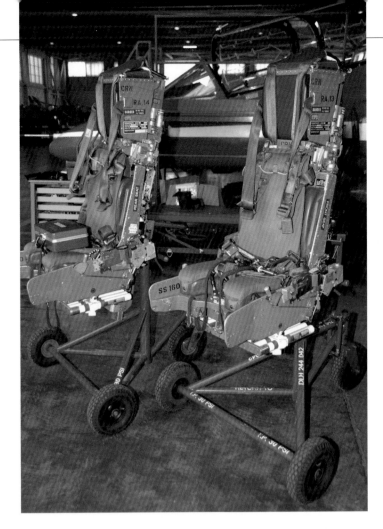

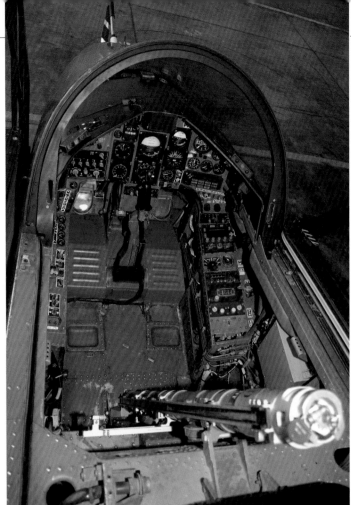

Λ During the July 2011 engineering break at Scampton, XX179 had both ejector seats removed for maintenance. They are seen here sitting on the special wheeled dollies. *(Keith Wilson)*

Λ The front cockpit of XX179 with the ejector seat removed. *(Keith Wilson)*

The role of the Junior Engineering Officer

For Flt Lt Adam Littler, joining the Red Arrows was his dream job. Having applied for the post of JEngO and being shortlisted, he underwent a two-day selection process in which all of the team had an input – everybody from Red 1 down to the Senior Aircraftsman (SAC). In his own words 'it allows many opportunities to represent the Air Force and to work with a great team of highly motivated individuals' and added as an afterthought, 'and you get to fly a lot, with Red 1!'

Adam's primary role is to lead the famous Red Arrows' Circus, a group of ten flight engineers, chosen annually on merit. Adam is the engineering officer in charge during all airshows and is the liaison between the Circus and the aircrew.

Red Arrows' Circus engineers

Each Red Arrows' pilot is allocated a specific Circus team member who remains with them throughout the season. Their role is to ensure that all the aircraft are refuelled, maintained and serviced, ready for the next display, while the aircraft are away from home. By way of a small compensation, they do get to fly in the backseat of the jets between shows and locations. If they are away from base for more

than three shows, the Red Arrows' Road Support Team – suitably qualified engineering personnel with tools and spares – are deployed to assist the Circus.

Adam relies heavily on his Circus Leader, usually a senior NCO, who is responsible for the day-to-day running of the Circus. For the 2011 season, the role was admirably filled by Sgt Matt Lord, in his second year with the Circus, whom Adam described as his 'Senior Subject Matter Expert' and regularly turned to him for advice. There is also a Deputy Circus Leader, usually a second-year Circus member, who is additionally responsible for all the documentation. The remaining Circus members are made up of Corporals and SACs from the three trades – Avionics, Mechanical and Armament (for the ejection seats).

While in Cyprus for the winter practice, each member of the Circus is responsible for maintaining his own aircraft. When on detachment, the Circus blues practise lots of 'formal starts' to ensure that the complete show, from engine start to shut-down, looks slick and efficient. They also undergo special sea and parachute drills (part of their annual safety training programme) as well as team-building activities. Once the Public Display Authority is approved by the AOC of 22 Group, the Circus are able to exchange their regular khaki overalls for the smart blue suits worn with pride at all the shows.

➤ At the same time as the seats where removed from XX179, the opportunity was taken to replace the Adour engine – seen here on an engine maintenance truck.
(Keith Wilson)

◄ This aircraft needs the starboard main undercarriage leg replaced and a team of four engineers – SAC Maria Cowie, SAC Kenny Walker, SAC James Smith and SAC Mark Pittaway – are seen manoeuvring the heavy and cumbersome leg into position.
(Keith Wilson)

➤ The two-week mid-season engineering break provides an opportunity to improve the cosmetic appearances of some of the aircraft. Here, the port intake is being masked ready for some new paintwork. The Red Arrows do not have painting staff on the team so specialist contractors are brought in to complete the task.
(Keith Wilson)

By the time of the mid-season engineering break in July 2011, the hours on the tailplane of XX306 had almost reached the limit so a decision was taken to change it. Here the aircraft is seen with its new tailplane awaiting fitting. _(Keith Wilson)_

Shortly afterwards, the engineers – Cpl Steve Forest, SAC Glen Jones, SAC Mark Cummings, SAC Adam Foster and SAC Kenny Walker – had the new tailplane fitted onto the aircraft and the back end of XX306 was ready to be reassembled. _(Keith Wilson)_

Hawk Replacement Programme

Officially titled 'Recovery from Storage of Hawk T1 aircraft and conversion to RAFAT Role', but better known as the Hawk Replacement Programme (HRP), it is operated at RAF Shawbury by civilian contractor FB Heliservices (FBH) – a joint venture between Bristow Helicopters Ltd (part of Bristow Group Inc) and Cobham Aviation Services (part of Cobham plc). FBH manages and operates the Aircraft Maintenance and Storage Unit at RAF Shawbury, as well as running the UK Defence Helicopter Flying School (DHFS) to provide training to all three services using a fleet of 36 AS350 Squirrels and 12 Bell 412EP Griffins, also at Shawbury.

The HRP is managed by John Dawson and features a small team of skilled, (mainly) former Air Force engineers led by supervisor Alan Tucker. The current plan is for three Hawk aircraft to be overhauled and handed over to the Reds for each of the next three years. This involves taking a suitable aircraft from storage and carrying out a major overhaul programme taking around 6,500 man hours. This is followed by a further modification programme to ensure that all modifications specific to their use with the Red Arrows (including the all-important smoke modifications) are carried out. For the first aircraft in the programme, the mods took 1,500 man-hours, but subsequent airframes are expected to take 1,300 man-hours each. Afterwards, the aircraft undergoes a full flight test at Shawbury (usually performed by Wing Commander David Firth-Wigglesworth, with Sqn Ldr Ross Priday in 'the boot') before being flown to RAF Cranwell for a complete respray in Red Arrows' colours.

It is a programme that appears to be operating efficiently and on-time, but Sqn Ldr Ross Priday puts much of that success down to the significant planning effort undertaken by FBH and the Reds, as well as excellent communications between the teams.

◄ **Nearing completion is XX323, the second aircraft in the Hawk Replacement Programme at RAF Shawbury. It has received a low-hour fin and rudder from former 100 Squadron aircraft XX345.**
(Keith Wilson)

➤ **XX323 has already been fitted with the red modified tail pipe containing the smoke generating pipes.**
(Keith Wilson)

➤ **The team has three survival equipment fitters who maintain all elements of the pilots' safety equipment. Cpl Dave Morris is seen testing one of the team's special aircrew life preservers and anti-g trousers on a test rig.**
(Keith Wilson)

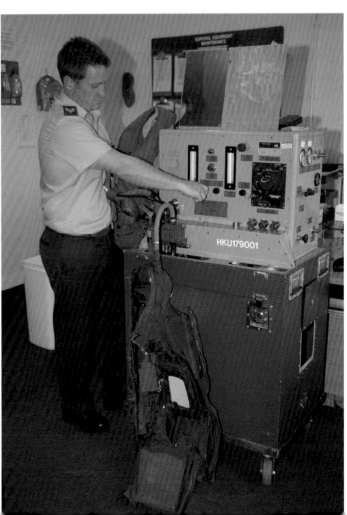

The second aircraft undergoing the programme is XX323 – a former RAF Valley aircraft – which is nearing completion having recently received a low-hours fin and rudder, donated by a former 100 Squadron aircraft, XX345.

Next aircraft undergoing the programme is XX219, which has been in storage at Shawbury for many years. It is now completely stripped and the overhaul is progressing well. The wings on XX219 were relatively high on both flying hours and FI so will be replaced with wings from XX185.

A couple of former Red Arrows' aircraft are in storage at Shawbury. XX294 operated with the team at Springhawk in 2010 before flying directly to Shawbury. The aircraft's airframe hours had reached a little over 8,137 and, more importantly, the fatigue life (150.568) had been met. A glance at the g-meter confirms that – showing 318 examples of 8g or more – a hard life indeed! Having been stripped of all key

Showtime!

Once the Public Display Authority has been issued and all team members have been authorised to wear their red or blue flying suits, the Red Arrows' display season is able to get underway. Ahead of the team are around 90 displays and more than 100 flypasts at a variety of events including airshows, national celebrations, sporting events, music festivals and community fêtes. In 2012, the Olympic Games will also offer an opportunity to showcase the very best of British with a Red Arrows' appearance.

The timetable is often busy and regularly the team will appear at two events on the same day, sometimes in different parts of Britain or Europe. With a full schedule of public appearances, each requiring thorough briefing and debriefing, it can be difficult to fit everything in. The engineers must work hard – often for long hours and in all types of weather – to ensure the requisite number of airframes is available for each display and transit. For flight safety purposes, it is also imperative that all flight and ground crew members have sufficient time to rest and recover for the following day's work.

The high level of planning and control required to ensure that – weather permitting – the Red Arrows arrive overhead at the appointed place at the appointed time is quite remarkable, especially when you consider just how small the team is that prepares and coordinates all this activity.

Behind the scenes at RAF Scampton is the Administration Team led by the team manager, Sqn Ldr Liz Parker, and supported by the team adjutant, WO Alan Murray, assisted by Sgt Buzz Matthews. In addition, a small Flight-planning Team – responsible for flight safety – provides the crew with aeronautical information and the latest weather reports.

Once the Red Arrows' display programme has been agreed for the season, detailed planning commences with a master file created for each and every event.

➤ **Sqn Ldr Ben Murphy (Red 1) leads the team off the ramp at Scampton, towards the taxiway and on to a display at RAF Waddington on 3 July. As the Circus is operating from its home base and not, on this occasion, in the public gaze, members are wearing their normal khaki and high-visibility jackets rather than their team-blue overalls.** *(Keith Wilson)*

Sqn Ldr Ben Murphy (Red 1) leads the team briefing ahead of the display at RAF Waddington on 3 July 2011. Note the wall clock accurately synchronised with a time signal transmitted from Rugby. *(Keith Wilson)*

When the team is away from home and the weather is suitable, the brief is held outside. Here the team is briefing ahead of the transit leg from Manston to Bristol on 14 August 2011. *(Crown Copyright/SAC Rob Travis)*

A member of the Dye Team carefully opens the valve on the red dye tap while listening to the liquid flowing in. *(Keith Wilson)*

The unique modifications fitted to the tail pipe of all Red Arrows' Hawk aircraft. The individual nozzles deliver white (diesel) plus red- and blue-coloured dye to the jet pipe; the heat from the jet exhaust does the rest. In addition to the coloured smoke adding to the viewers' enjoyment of the show, it provides an important safety aid to the formation flying. *(Keith Wilson)*

All in a week's work

Take a 'typical' week in 2011, covering the Red Arrows' activities from 4–8 August: the schedule included three ISPs at Scampton, followed by displays at Swanage (Dorset), Newcastle (Northern Ireland), Cowes (Isle of Wight), Rhyl and Blackpool, and mandatory simulator training at RAF Valley for the pilots before returning to Scampton. The events required a ten-aircraft 'push' to all venues; a Red Arrows' Road Team to Bournemouth for two nights; a Dye Team to Hawarden for two nights; and a PR Team to Blackpool for two nights.

Timing sheet The planning process starts with the Team Manager producing a timing sheet for every display activity. The key moment at each location is the display start time (always agreed with the airshow organiser well in advance) and around this the departure from base, transit time as planned and calculated by the pilot responsible for that leg of the route, display timings and transit back to base are factored in. That is the plan for the first event but, before you can move on the next one, the aircraft need to be refuelled and loaded with the smoke-generating diesel and dye from the Dye Team. This process is known simply as the 'turnaround' and, normally, a minimum of 1 hour 45 minutes is allowed, although a little longer is preferred and appreciated by all involved.

Fuel requirements can also be calculated at this stage, based on the known timings, and the Circus team members ensure the correct amount is loaded into each jet.

Navigator In addition, the timing document is also used to allocate a designated pilot as navigator for a particular sector as the task is shared among the Team members.

What's Happening Manager? With all this information factored in for the five days, accurate timings for all aspects of the 'push' will now be available. It is at this point in the planning that the WHAM? (What's Happening Manager?) document comes to the forefront. The Team Adjutant then calculates *all* other details around those timings, including those for road transport (for the MT team), the Dye Team, WHAM? Check Meeting (for all involved), Met brief, main briefing, video timings (essential for every display) as well as Red 10's timings. WHAM? also includes timings for the Squirrel helicopters provided by the Central Flying School (Helicopters) based at RAF Shawbury required to position the airshow commentator (Red 10) and the Video Team into position ahead of displays at events away from major airfields.

WHAM? includes all accommodation details and telephone details of any agencies the team may need to contact. In summary, it is a masterpiece in micro-planning and one of the key items that ensures the Red Arrows appear so slick.

What's Happening in PR Next in the planning process comes the WHIPR (What's Happening in PR) document, which provides a similar level of detail for all those involved in supporting the Red Arrows in public – for the weekend in question it covered the Red Arrows' tent and PR personnel at the Blackpool event for two days.

When the Circus is preparing the aircraft for a show, there is no time to spare. Here, the junior engineering officer and Circus 1 (Flt Lt Adam Littler) is seen cleaning Red 1's Hawk jet ahead of the ISP at Scampton on 5 August 2011. *(Keith Wilson)*

Flt Lt David Montenegro (Red 6) is assisted with strapping into his jet by Cpl Jamie Hatcher (Blue 6) at Scampton on 3 July 2011, ahead of the display at RAF Waddington. *(Keith Wilson)*

Red Arrows' team leader Sqn Ldr Ben Murphy (Red 1) marches across the ramp at Scampton towards his jet, ahead of the ISP on 5 August 2011. *(Keith Wilson)*

➢ All the activities of the Circus are precise and carefully choreographed on the ramp ahead of a display. Once the pilots have been strapped into the jets and the aircraft checked, all the Blues wait at the nose of their aircraft as the cockpits are closed ready for engine start. This is a strict safety precaution to protect the ground crew from (a very remote possibility of) an inadvertent firing of the miniature detonating cords embedded in the perspex canopy. *(Keith Wilson)*

➢ Once the engine has been started and ear defenders fitted, further safety checks are conducted by the aircraft's Circus Team member. Here Circus 2 – SAC Geraldine Beaton – carries out those checks on the jet of Red 2 (Flt Lt Chris Lyndon-Smith) on the ramp at Scampton on 5 August 2011 just before the ISP. *(Oliver Wilson)*

➢ The signals may look a little odd, but they each have a clear purpose. Here, the Circus Blues are signalling the position of the flaps to the pilots during the checks. Nearest the camera is Sgt Matt Lord (Circus 8) signalling to Red 8 (Flt Lt Dave Davies). *(Keith Wilson)*

◄ The signalling continues. Cpl Dave Howard (Circus 3) indicates the position of the flaps to Red 3 (Flt Lt Sean Cunningham). *(Keith Wilson)*

◄ Once all the checks have been completed, the Circus members position themselves to the front left of the aircraft nose and await a signal from Circus 1 to leave the ramp. *(Keith Wilson)*

◄ Once the signal has been given, Circus members march from the aircraft and position themselves on the edge of the ramp so that they can complete last-chance checks as the aircraft taxi directly towards them before turning and heading onto the taxiway. *(Keith Wilson)*

Red 1, Sqn Ldr Ben Murphy, leads the team off the ramp at Scampton before the In Season Display Practice (ISP) on 5 August 2011, with members of the Circus looking on for last-chance checks on each aircraft. (Keith Wilson)

The last-chance checks. As the Reds taxi away from the ramp, all the Circus team members keep a careful eye on each of the aircraft. (Oliver Wilson)

Red 10, the display manager

Then there is the role of Red 10, the display manager, who does not only provide the sparkling commentary at all full displays. For the 2009, 2010 and 2011 display seasons, the job was undertaken by Sqn Ldr Graeme Bagnall, a former Tornado GR4 pilot with three tours and more than 2,000 fast jet hours' experience. Red 10 also has a supervisory role in the squadron as the day-to-day supervisor of flying and training, working alongside Red 11.

Red 10 has to be on the ground at every display and provides the eyes and ears for Red 1. Graeme reckons that the public role of show commentator occupies less than 5% of his time. A greater proportion of his time is spent coordinating with all the flying display directors, flying controllers and the Flying Control Committee (often referred to as 'The Air Police') right across the team's air display programme – refining the fine detail that makes everything happen according to the plan.

Let us look at a 'typical' display for Sqn Ldr Graeme Bagnall. On 17 August 2011, the Red Arrows were scheduled to appear at the Cromer Carnival – a cliff-top display at the picturesque Norfolk location. The team have been regular visitors to this annual event and always feature at the top of the bill. Their attendance, along with some pleasant summer weather, attracted large crowds to the event which, unfortunately, caused traffic jams in the surrounding areas. It's known as the 'Red Arrows Effect'.

Graeme arrived at Scampton as normal and after checking all the day's arrangements and the latest Met forecast he climbed into a Squirrel HC2 for the journey to Cromer. He was accompanied by Cpl

◅ **Everything about the Red Arrows is precise, even taxiing, as clearly demonstrated during a departure for practice at Akrotiri on 20 May 2010.** (EJ van Koningsveld)

⋀ **Defence Helicopter Flying School Aerospatiale AS350B2 Ecureuil G-DOIT/99 arriving onto the Cromer cliff top with team commentator Sqn Ldr Graeme Bagnall (Red 10) and team photographer Cpl Graham Taylor on board – in readiness for the Cromer Carnival display on 17 August 2011.** (Keith Wilson)

Graham Taylor, who was to record the entire display on video for the subsequent debrief. After having arrived at Cromer, the helicopter flew up and down the display area to check from the air, then it landed on the cliff top, right on time. After landing, Graeme met the display organiser and inspected the entire site – satisfying himself that the crowd lines and car parks would not interfere with the display. He also checked the funfair to make sure the larger rides would not become hazards. Graeme then moved to the cliff top and using his portable meteorological equipment checked the surface wind and atmospheric pressure to ascertain the site QFE, which provides a datum point for 'zero' height on the Hawks' altimeters. As the site is on top of the cliffs, the number obtained is adjusted downwards to make allowance for the actual barometric pressure at sea level.

Next on the task list was a call to Red 1. The decision on whether to fly at the event or not, was made. The site is considered either 'fit' or 'unfit'; there is no in-between. Thankfully, for all the visitors to the show, it was declared 'fit'. Next, and after taking all the known weather information into account, an initial decision is made on the type of display to be flown: Flat, Rolling or Full Show. With virtually clear skies and little change expected, it was to be a Full Show. This decision can be changed at any time before or even during the show, if the weather changes significantly – particularly the height of the cloud base. Finally, Graeme concludes the conversation with a detailed site briefing, mentioning anything that might affect the display, including the location of any high objects such as the funfair. Red 1 confirms that the show will go ahead, as planned.

⋀ **Immediately after landing, Red 10, Sqn Ldr Graeme Bagnall, checked the weather conditions and the site security before calling the team leader, Red 1. Ultimately, it is Red 10's responsibility to ensure the safety, integrity and suitability of all display sites.**
(Keith Wilson)

➤ **Just one important part of the Red Arrows' logistical support is their large, articulated transporter, seen loading a weekend's show material and support equipment at Scampton on 3 July 2011 ahead of a major push to Koksijde in Belgium.**
(Keith Wilson)

◁ Part of the Circus support material stored at the back of the hangar at Scampton in readiness for the next push. In the front are the special equipment bags used by each of the team and to the right are the fuselage luggage panniers. All equipment is numbered from one to ten, to correspond to each of the aircraft involved in the push. *(Keith Wilson)*

◁ There is very little baggage space available in the Hawk jet, only a small bay under the fuselage where a special luggage pannier is fitted. Cpl Kevin Smith loads pannier number 5 into Red 5 at Scampton on 5 August 2011 ahead of the push to Bournemouth (twice), Aldergrove and Hawarden, for a busy weekend of shows at Swanage, Newcastle (NI), Cowes, Rhyl, Blackpool and Minehead – as well as a series of flypasts. *(Keith Wilson)*

⋁ Getting the pannier into the fuselage underside bay is a tricky job, before making sure it is strapped-in and secure for the flight – although Cpl Kevin Smith makes it look easy. *(Keith Wilson)*

With about 45 minutes before the Red Arrows will appear from behind the crowd in their typically dynamic manner, all that is left for Graeme is about 30 minutes of PR work – at the event, he is the face of the team.

With minutes to go before the arrival time, Graeme positions himself on the elevated show commentator's stand, PA microphone in one hand and two-way radio in the other. The two-way radio, tuned to the Red Arrows' display frequency, means he is in direct contact with the team once they are close to the area. While the obvious reason is that they can advise him when they are just a couple of minutes from entering the display area, there is another – far more important – safety reason for the radio. The team is provided with temporary restricted airspace (TRA) of 6 nautical miles (11km), centred on the display datum, from ground level up to 8,000ft (2,438m) to protect it from unwanted incursions from other aircraft during shows. While the protected airspace is published by NOTAMs (the Civil Aviation Authorities Notices to Airman), not all pilots read them or understand them. If Graeme were to spot a conflicting aircraft or helicopter, he would immediately be able to communicate it to Red 1, who would be able to make a decision on whether to suspend the display and recommence it when the incursion has cleared away or, as in the case at Silverstone in 2010, immediately terminate the show completely and give the order for all nine aircraft to return to Scampton. On this occasion at least 33 unwanted aircraft and helicopters broke the TRA and many became serious safety hazards. No such problems at Cromer.

⋀ **One of the team's photographers must be on hand at each show to record the event on video in order to allow the team to de-brief after the particular event. The rule is quite simple: no video – no show! Here, Cpl Graham Taylor is recording the ISP at Scampton on 5 August 2011 from 'show centre', right in front of the air traffic control building.** (Keith Wilson)

➢ **The team usually starts a show with a liberal dose of red, white and blue smoke on the take-off roll. They are caught in the act while practising at Akrotiri in May 2009.** (EJ van Koningsveld)

⚤ With very little space available in the Hawk jets, the ground crews have discovered innovative ways to keep their drinks cool while the aircraft is in transit. *(Keith Wilson)*

➤ Red 10 (Sqn Ldr Graeme Bagnall) in action at Lowestoft during the Red Arrows' seaside display on 12 August 2011. Positioned at the end of the pier and in contact with the team via the radio, Graeme provided a sparkling commentary for the Red Arrows' display along the seafront. *(Keith Wilson)*

The Red Arrows arrived on time, from the rear of the crowd, with their red, blue and white display smoke prominent. They continued their performance over the water and Graeme delivered his sparkling commentary for the 24 minutes of the team's full display. All too soon, it was over. Near-silence descended on the cliff tops while the smell of red, white and blue smoke hung in the air for a few minutes, until it was blown out to sea. Over the PA, Graeme hoped the large crowd had enjoyed the Reds and thanked them for coming to the show. He, along with the Red Arrows, received a rapturous applause.

He had a few moments for conversations with the visitors and signing a few photographs before both he and Graham Taylor made their way back to the waiting helicopter for the return trip to Scampton – Red 1 would be waiting expectantly in the briefing room at Scampton for the tape of the display in order to complete the team's debrief.

Once back at Scampton, was Graeme's day over? Absolutely not! He had to go through the process again with a transit down to Bournemouth for a display at Weymouth later in the day. Graeme's task in this transit was to fly the spare Hawk, Red 10, with the main formation. Then it was another helicopter trip to and from Weymouth for a seaside show, before returning to Bournemouth Airport, as the team had shows at the Dawlish Carnival and the Fowey Royal Regatta the following day.

⋀ **The team in action just off the beach at Lowestoft on 12 August 2011 – running in for the Whirlwind manoeuvre in loose Diamond formation. The seafront shows provide a great spectacle for the visitors who have a marvellous view of the team from along the beach.** (Keith Wilson)

➤ **The Red Arrows always start their show with a spectacular entrance from behind the crowd, as they did at the Cromer Carnival on 17 August 2011. Unusually though, the lead aircraft – Red 1 – was the 'spare' black Hawk (XX284) lent to the team for the show season by RAF Valley. As it does not have any smoke-making equipment, it can only fly in the lead position. Cpl Graham Taylor was in position to record the event on video for the post-flight briefing.** (Crown Copyright/ SAC Dan Herrick)

Is there a better way to view the Red Arrows than from the cockpit of an aircraft in close formation with them? The Red Arrows running in at the start of a show practice over Akrotiri on 14 May 2011. *(EJ van Koningsveld)*

The pilots' public role

While the Red Arrows' air display is in great demand, so are the pilots. At many of the larger shows, members of the team make public appearances for the visiting public – and very well attended and appreciated these are. At the bigger shows – such as the Royal International Air Tattoo at Fairford – the aircraft are based on site over the weekend so public appearances are relatively easy. Such is the demand for their time that the team have to split up into smaller groups to visit the various locations and sponsors who had 'invited' them. It cannot be easy, after having flown a physically and mentally demanding formation performance, to turn on the charm, smile and meet the public. But they do, and they do it extremely well. Their ability to have a smile for everyone, especially the younger audience, and a pleasant answer to even the daftest question is remarkable. The author shadowed the Red Arrows at various events and it never ceased to impress him just how hard the team works – not just the pilots, but *all* the team.

At the Airbourne Show at Eastbourne in August 2011, the team performed displays on all three days of the seaside event while operating from Manston Airport, Kent. Airbourne has become the largest seaside show in the UK and probably anywhere else for that matter. The appearance of the Red Arrows' team on the ground later in the day brought very large crowds to the display arena. They spent around an hour touring the arena, meeting people and signing photographs and leaflets, before meeting local dignitaries and sponsors. They even had time for a short game of football with some young boys from nearby Brighton Football Club – all in aid of charity. They always seem to have time and nothing appears to be too much trouble.

◄ **Another well-attended seaside venue is the Airbourne Eastbourne 2011 show – the world's biggest free seafront airshow. Operating from Manston, Kent, the Red Arrows headlined both weekend shows. Here, the Enid section of the team is seen passing over Eastbourne Pier ahead of the Rollback manoeuvre, 13 August.** (Keith Wilson)

▲ **Occasionally, the crew's flight safety equipment is hurriedly removed at the end of a show and left on the wing of the jet for the ground crew to attend to, as here when Red 6 (Flt Lt David Montenegro) was required to climb into a helicopter and fly the short distance to the Waddington Airshow so that he, along with all the Red Arrows' team members, could make a public appearance at the show.** (Keith Wilson)

△ At the end of their flying display on 3 July 2011, five members of the Red Arrows' team are air lifted from Scampton back to Waddington so that they can make an important public appearance at the show. A similar helicopter took the remaining team members to the event. The Defence Helicopter Flying School regularly provides the Red Arrows with Aerospatiale Squirrel HT1 helicopters for this task. *(Keith Wilson)*

▽ The public appearance of the Red Arrows in the show arena at Eastbourne's Airbourne 2011 event, shortly after their display along the seafront, was eagerly awaited. Here seven members of the Reds are working their way around the arena on 13 August. Left to right: Flt Lt Sean Cunningham (Red 3), Sqn Ldr Ross Priday (SEngO), Sqn Ldr Ben Murphy (Red 1), Flt Lt David Montenegro (Red 6), Flt Lt Ben Plank (Red 7), Flt Lt David Davies (Red 8) and Flt Lt Kirsty Stewart (Red 5). *(Keith Wilson)*

➢ A moment in his life this young man will never forget – posing with three members of the world's premier formation aerobatic display team. Six-year-old Morgan Howcroft, suitably dressed in his own Red Arrows' flying suit, 'signs' a poster while posing on the Royal Air Force Association stand at RIAT with Sqn Ldr Ben Murphy (Red 1), Flt Lt Jon Egging (Red 4) and Flt Lt Chris Lyndon-Smith (Red 2). *(Keith Wilson)*

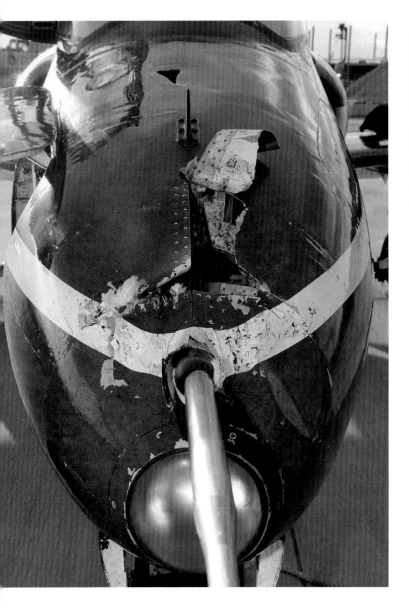

◁ **Flt Lt David Montenegro (Red 2) suffered a bird strike in XX227 while displaying at Gibraltar in 2009, but landed the aircraft without further incident. The bird went right through the nose of the aircraft and some of the feathers are visible just behind the probe.** *(Crown Copyright/Cpl Ralph Merry)*

↖ **Looking up through the nose undercarriage bay, the remains of the bird are clearly visible.** *(Crown Copyright/Cpl Ralph Merry)*

Bird strike!

Seaside shows have become very popular in the UK. Most are free (or relatively inexpensive) and the crowds that turn out to watch are large. A quick look down the calendar for 2011 shows the team displayed at seaside events at Southend, Margate, Southport, Blackpool, Lowestoft, Cromer, Weymouth, Bournemouth, Clacton, Morecombe and Eastbourne. Many of these venues have become annual seaside shows.

They provide great opportunities for the team to display to large audiences, although they present an additional hazard to the display aircraft – seabirds. The risk of bird strikes near the sea is significantly higher and while the team does take all possible precautions, occasionally bird strikes do occur. Sometimes the damage and consequences are limited, other times they can be more serious.

For Ben Plank, displaying Red 7 (XX266) along Blackpool Pleasure Beach on 7 August 2011 will live long in his memory. He takes up the story:

"Having completed a display at the Blackpool pleasure beach I was chasing down the main formation. After Monty (Red 6) and I have finished our Synchro routine we pitch behind the crowd to allow the remaining seven jets to complete their final break. After that Monty and I fly either side of the crowd and catch the main formation up. As I was passing over the coast and travelling at around 450kts at 300ft I looked across to pick Monty up on the coastline; he was trailing white smoke to allow me to visually acquire him. At that moment a brown flash passed by the canopy shortly followed by the loudest bang I have ever heard. The jet started vibrating and the central warning panel (a series of emergency lights that illuminate telling the pilot something is wrong) lit up like a Christmas tree! I rolled the jet level and pulled into a climb to get away from the ground. The T6NL caution had lit indicating the engine was in surge so I selected idle which cleared the caution. The engine was still vibrating and when I looked back inside the cockpit to check the engine indication I noted that it was

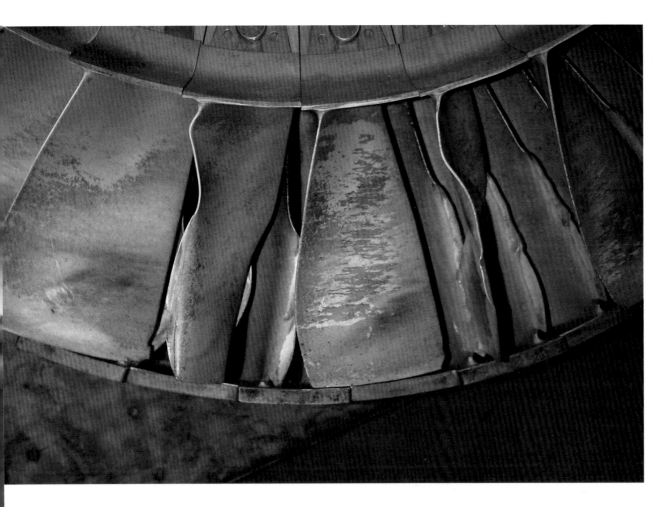

◁ **Badly damaged engine blades on the Adour 102 after Flt Lt Ben Plank's bird strike incident at Blackpool in XX260 on 7 August 2011. The aircraft was removed from Blackpool on a low-loader and taken to Shawbury where it was subsequently withdrawn from service.** *(Rolls-Royce)*

flaming out and winding down. I relit the engine and crossed my fingers that it would work. While I waited (hoped!) for the engine to spool back up I put out a radio call 'Fly it through, Red 7 bird strike engine failure'. The 'fly it through' call is always made to the Boss if you have an emergency and it also allows the navigating pilot (the team member selected to plan and coordinate that particular show) to alert air traffic control of the problem. Zane Sennett (Red 9) made a Mayday call to Blackpool, the nearest airfield which was fortunately a few miles to the south of my position.

I was relieved to see both the RPM and turbine gas temperature steadily rising and although the engine was still sounding a little unwell and vibrating it appeared to be back on line. I switched my attention to landing at Blackpool. With only one engine that was clearly badly damaged I elected to fly a glide approach into the airport in case the engine subsequently failed. In the mean time Monty had flown back to offer any assistance. Blackpool ATC had cleared me to land on any runway and I positioned the aircraft through the overhead. I updated the formation stating that I had successfully re-lit the engine and turned my smoke on to reduce my landing mass (weight). The runway at Blackpool was not particularly long and the run-off at the far end is straight into the sand dunes so I needed to land at the correct speed close to the threshold. I lowered the gear and flap; I had been passed my landing clearance by Red

9 and tracked just short of the runway to allow a last-minute flare to touch me down at the start of the runway. At around 300ft the engine started to vibrate more but I was confident that I had enough energy to glide onto the runway. Once I touched down Monty overshot to rejoin the other seven jets and I called to the Boss that I was safely on the deck. I had selected idle on touch-down and the engine had started to vibrate even more. I used my roll-out speed to vacate the runway and brought the jet to a stop.

Then there was an almighty bang as the front stage of the compressor sheered off the rest of the engine . . . it had failed! I jumped out to be met by the fire teams that had been scrambled to assist. I peered down the intake to see significant engine damage."

Ben Plank makes it sound so simple. It wasn't! The engine was written off and the aircraft transferred to RAF Shawbury by road after the incident. Ben's next display at the Minehead Summer Festival a few days later was in a different jet. XX266 was destined not to fly again.

The Red Arrows are probably the best jet aerobatic display team in the world. They are wonderful ambassadors for everything British. The have been and still are a great recruitment tool for the Royal Air Force. And they have time for everyone.

What is the secret of their success for all these years? Simple – it is down to great planning, perfect execution and an impeccable smile!

The 1977 season was dominated by the Queen's Silver Jubilee celebrations and the team's Gnat T1s were part of the mass flypast over Buckingham Palace on 11 June.

The Red Arrows gave their last display with the Folland Gnat at RAF Valley on 15 September 1979. By this time, they had given 1,292 displays and visited 18 countries. All of the 12 remaining Gnat T1s in use with the team were withdrawn from service and allocated to ground duties.

Ambassadors abroad for the Hawk

In 1983, now equipped with Hawk T1 aircraft, the team embarked on its second tour of North America. Retracing the route taken by the 1972 team and once again supported by a pair of Hercules C1 aircraft, the Red Arrows left Scampton on 3 May and arrived at Trenton AFB, Ontario, two days later – a significantly quicker journey than that taken by the Gnats 11 years earlier.

The main display of the tour was at the Andrews AFB Armed Forces Day where the 100th anniversary of manned flight was being celebrated. A crowd in excess of 700,000, in addition to coast-to-coast television viewers, watched the 20-minute display. The F-16s of the USAF Demonstration Team, the Thunderbirds, were also at event, making their first public appearance since the accident that had killed four of their pilots the previous January. The Red Arrows also gave displays at Charleston, North Carolina, and at the US Navy Academy at Annapolis, Maryland, on 23 May, where they shared the bill with the US Navy's A-4 Skyhawk-equipped Blue Angels display team. Returning through Canada, the chance to meet all three of the North American display teams was realised when the Red Arrows got together with the Canadian Air Force's Snowbirds and their Canadair Tutors at Bagotville.

In June 1986 the team departed on a six-week, 17-nation tour of the Far East. They travelled 18,800 miles (30,255km) and completed 22 displays, without any cancellations due to bad weather or serviceability. Named Easter Express, the deployment of 11 Hawks and 2 Hercules support aircraft visited Germany, Switzerland, Italy, Egypt, Saudi Arabia, Oman, Jordan, India, Malaysia, Thailand, Singapore and Indonesia. It is interesting to compare the tour schedule with the names of customers who went on to order and operate the Hawk aircraft.

Displays worldwide in the 1990s

In June 1990, an historic visit was made to the then Soviet Union when the team flew to Leningrad (today's St Petersburg), and carried out two displays over the Ukrainian capital, Kiev, in support of the British Trade Fair. They were not allowed to fly or perform near Moscow, but they did carry out two shows from a sport-flying and sky-diving centre at Chaika, close to the capital. On the return journey, they went via Hungary and displayed at Budapest, watched by a large crowd.

Although declared temporarily homeless due to the closure of RAF Scampton as a result of the Government's defence cuts, the team departed on a five-month, 50,000-mile (80,465km) promotional tour of South Africa, Australia and the Far East in September 1995. The trip was sponsored by ten British defence companies and the first part of the 23-nation tour went via the Middle East and Africa, where they took part in the celebrations for the 75th anniversary of the South African Air Force.

The second part of the tour took them to southern and southeast Asia, where they performed in Malaysia at LIMA 95 (the Langkawi International Maritime and Aerospace Exhibition). In mid-January, they arrived in Australia, where their performance over Sydney Harbour attracted an audience of 1.2 million people. After displays in Brunei and the Philippines, the Red Arrows performed at the Asian Aerospace 96 Air Show in Singapore. On the journey back to the UK, they displayed in Bangkok before returning to their new home at RAF Cranwell.

Another tour of the Middle and Far East was arranged for the team in November 1999. The six-week deployment saw the Red Arrows' display at the Dubai 2000 International Air Show and the opening of LIMA 99 in Malaysia.

Flying into the new millennium

In 2002, a short trip was organised to Canada, but this deployment led to the cancellation of 14 shows in the UK. The tour included three displays at the Canadian International Air Show in Toronto, during which time they flew with the Canadair CT-114s of the Canadian Forces Demonstration Team, the Snowbirds. On the journey home, the two teams met up again at the Nova Scotia International Air Show in Shearwater.

▼ **In June 1990, an historic first visit is made to the then Soviet Union when the Red Arrows fly to Leningrad (today's St Petersburg) and later mount two displays over the Ukrainian capital, Kiev, in support of the British Trade Fair. They also carry out a photo shoot against the backdrop of the Mother Motherland Monument in the centre of Kiev. The return journey is made by crossing the border into Hungary and completing the team's third and final display of the short tour at Budapest.** _(Crown Copyright)_

➤ **The team departs on a five-month, 50,000-mile tour of South Africa, Australia and the Far East in September 1995, sponsored by British defence companies. In mid-January 1996, they arrive in Australia and perform over Sydney Harbour Bridge. The tour is a commercial success with British Aerospace gaining a number of orders for the Hawk from countries visited during the trip.** _(Crown Copyright)_

◁ To mark the retirement of the RAF's last Avro Vulcan, the team flies in formation with XH558 at the Cranfield Airshow in September 1992. *(Crown Copyright)*

➤ British Airways Concorde G-BOAD in formation with the Red Arrows over the Wash, 29 May 2002, during a practice for the Queen's Golden Jubilee Flypast on 4 June. The Concorde was flown by Captain Mike Bannister and was photographed from Red 11 – Hawk XX227 – flown by Wg Cdr Bill Ramsey. *(EJ van Koningsveld)*

◄ **Above and below: During a short visit to Canada in 2002, the Red Arrows make a formation flight with the Canadian Air Force's Snowbirds team. After taking off from Halifax International Airport, the photo shoot is conducted along Canada's east coast. The cameraship is Red 10 – XX227 – flown by Flt Lt Steve Underwood.** *(EJ van Koningsveld)*

One of the highlights of the 2002 season was the formation fly-past over Buckingham Palace for the Queen's Golden Jubilee Celebrations on 4 June, in company with British Airway's Concorde G-BOAD.

In September 2003, as part of Exercise Eastern Hawk, the team visited ten countries in the Middle East and Far East. The tour was supported by both BAe Systems and Rolls-Royce. With the advent of digital photography, the photographic coverage of the event was significant and photo shoots were arranged over the spectacular Palm Island resort and the luxurious Burj Al Arab hotel along the Dubai Shoreline. The tour travelled to Malaysia and on 15 October a photographic flight took place over the city of Putrajaya, including the stunning Putra Mosque.

⋎ **The Red Arrows make a formation fly-by with a USAF F-117 Nighthawk, flown by RAF exchange pilot Sqn Ldr Richie Matthews, at the Royal International Air Tattoo at Fairford on 19 July 2003.** (Peter R. March)

➤ **After an interval of nine years, the team once again visit Canada, in 2002. The short tour includes three displays at the Canadian International Airshow in Toronto, as well as a photo shoot over Niagara Falls.** (Crown Copyright)

On 15 October 2003, as part of Eastern Hawk 03, the team makes a photographic flight over the Putra Mosque in Putrajaya, Malaysia. *(Crown Copyright/Cpl Chris Ward)*

Both show days at the July 2005 Royal International Air Tattoo see a spectacular formation to highlight the 'surveillance' theme, with the Red Arrows leading three Photo Reconnaissance Spitfires operated by the Battle of Britain Memorial Flight, Rolls-Royce and Peter Teichman. *(Crown Copyright/Cpl Andy Benson)*

The Red Arrows fly across the Tyne Bridge at the start of the 2004 Great North Run on 26 September. *(Crown Copyright /Cpl Andy Benson)*

The 40th display season

The year 2004 marked the team's official 40th display season. After the Public Display Authority had been awarded at the conclusion of their training programme at Akrotiri, the team performed at Marka in Jordan and Cognac, France, on their way back to the UK. Their official anniversary was marked with a private event at RAF Cranwell on 21 May with two former team members – Ray Hanna and Henry Prince – on the guest list. They celebrated the anniversary by incorporating a privately owned Folland Gnat (G-BVPP/XP534), masquerading as 'XR993' and flown by Sqn Ldr Willie Hackett, into the first manoeuvre of the display.

The 2006 season began with a three-week goodwill tour of the Far East, Middle East and Europe. Once again sponsored by a number of British defence companies, the tour was organised with a view to promoting British industry in the regions and the Red Arrows were accompanied by a BAe Systems Hawk 128 for much of the trip. Eight countries were visited: Jordan, India, Oman, Abu Dhabi, Bahrain, Saudi Arabia, Greece and Spain.

Another six-week tour of the Middle and Far East was organised for November 2007 – once again, with the assistance of BAe Systems

◄ During a flypast at Biggin Hill on 3 September 2005, the Red Arrows are joined by three aircraft representing RAF formation display teams from the past: the Gnat, in Yellowjacks colours, and a pair of Hunters – one in Black Arrows colours and the other Blue Diamond colours. *(Peter R. March)*

⋀ The team's 2006 display season begins with a three-week goodwill tour of the Far East, Middle East and Europe. Here, the Reds and a BAe Systems Hawk 128 fly past Bahrain on 28 May. *(Crown Copyright/Cpl Andy Benson)*

⋀ This unusual formation of nine Red Arrows' Hawks and six Blue Angels' FA-18s is made during both teams' visits to the Leeuwarden Air Force Base, Holland, 16 June 2006. Cameraship is a CFS Hawk, XX294, flown by Sqn Ldr W Wesley. *(EJ van Koningsveld)*

➤ **The Red Arrows undertake a six-week tour of the Middle and Far East in November 2007 – Exercise Eastern Arrow 2007. Supported by BAe Systems and Rolls-Royce, they visit 13 countries and fly 15,000 miles (24,140km) before returning to the UK. One port of call is Dubai where the Reds are photographed on 7 November.** *(Crown Copyright/Cpl Andy Benson)*

◄ **The 40th anniversary of the VC-10 entering service with the Royal Air Force – on 7 June 1966 – is marked at the Royal International Air Tattoo on 16 July 2006 when a specially painted VC-10 C1K, XV104 of No 101 Squadron is joined by the Red Arrows.** *(Peter R March)*

A In September and October 2003 – supported by British industry, including BAe Systems and Rolls-Royce – the team visits ten countries in the Middle East and Far East as part of Exercise Eastern Hawk 03. Returning via Egypt, they perform at Giza and became the first aerobatic display team to be allowed to display over the pyramids. *(BAe)*

◁ In November 2007, the Red Arrows make a 15,000-mile (24,140km) goodwill tour of the Middle East and Far East. During the six-week Exercise 'Eastern Arrow 2007', the team visit 14 countries and perform 16 displays in, among others, Jordan, Saudi Arabia, Dubai, Qatar, Oman, Malaysia and Abu Dhabi. While in Dubai, the team fly in formation with Emirates' Boeing 777-31H, A6-EMP on 14 November. *(Crown Copyright/Cpl Andy Benson)*

↑ **While on the six-week 'Eastern Arrow 2007' tour, the team visit Langkawi, Malaysia, where they fly in formation with Air Asia Airbus A330-301, 9M-XAA.** *(Crown Copyright/Cpl Andy Benson)*

➤ **The team fly in formation with Etihad Airways' Airbus A340-642, A6-EHE, as part of 'Eastern Arrow 2007', Dubai, 15 December.** *(Crown Copyright/Cpl Andy Benson)*

In June and July 2008, the Red Arrows return to the United States and Canada on a tour codenamed Exercise 'Western Arrow 2008'. *(Crown Copyright/SAC Ben Stephenson)*

As part of 'Western Arrow 2008', on 25 June the team conducts a photographic flight around a number of New York landmarks, including the Statue of Liberty...

⋀ ...and the Verrazano-Narrows Bridge connecting Brooklyn to Staten Island...

⋁ ... and downtown New York.
(All photographs, Crown Copyright/ SAC Ben Stevenson)

⋁ **The Red Arrows fly over Providence, Rhode Island, 25 June 2008.**
(Crown Copyright/ SAC Ben Stevenson)

and Rolls-Royce. This time the team visited 13 countries and flew 15,000 miles (24,140 km) before returning to the UK on 18 December. The PR machine was in full swing during this trip and the Red Arrows were photographed in formation with an Emirates' Boeing 777 over Dubai, an Air Asia Airbus A330 over Langkawi, Malaysia, and an Etihad Airways' Airbus A340, once again over Dubai.

Celebrating the RAF's 90th anniversary

The 90th anniversary of the Royal Air Force was celebrated on 1 April 2008 with a major fly past over London and the Red Arrows were joined by four new Eurofighter Typhoons for their slot in the mass formation.

Later that year, in June and July, the Red Arrows returned to the United States and Canada for a tour codenamed Exercise Western Arrow 2008. They were supported by a Boeing C-17A Globemaster III from 99 Squadron and arranged the obligatory formation photo shoot on the trip. While in New York, they also used the opportunity to arrange a photographic tour around a number of local landmarks, including the Statue of Liberty, the Verrazano-Narrows Bridge and downtown New York, before passing over Providence, Rhode Island.

This trip marked the last of the major tours, although the Red Arrows have been busy with a large number of displays in the UK and Europe since then.

At the time of writing, the Red Arrows have performed more than 4,400 displays in 54 different countries – proving excellent ambassadors for the Royal Air Force and the United Kingdom wherever they venture.

⋀ **The 90th Anniversary of the Royal Air Force is celebrated on 1 April 2008 with a major fly-by over London. Four Eurofighter Typhoons join the Red Arrows for the formation.** *(Crown Copyright/Cpl Andy Benson)*

⋁ **In June and July 2008, the Red Arrows return to the United States and Canada on a tour codenamed Exercise 'Western Arrow 2008', supported by a No 99 Squadron Boeing C-17A Globemaster III, ZZ176. A formation photograph was obtained on 25 June.** *(Crown Copyright/ SAC Ben Stevenson)*

◄ The Red Arrows have appeared in Gibraltar on seven occasions, including 2009 when they made a display appearance on 18 September. This shot of the team in battle formation was taken on their arrival the previous evening. *(Crown Copyright/ Junior Technician Shayne Humphrey)*

∨ A formation flown over the Jersey Airshow on 9 September 2010, just after the Vulcan had provided its solo performance and just before the Reds flew their routine. *(Crown Copyright/SAC(T) James Smith)*

Jon Egging

On the 20 August 2011, Flt Lt Jon Egging (Red 4) tragically lost his life while completing a display at the Bournemouth Air Festival. He was coming to the end of his first year with the RAF Red Arrows aerobatic team.

Having developed a love of flying at an early age, Jon joined the Royal Air Force in 2000. Selected for fast jet training, Jon flew the Tucano and the Hawk before becoming a Qualified Flying Instructor on the Hawk at RAF Valley, teaching both students and instructors. Jon went on to serve with IV (AC) Squadron – 'Happy IV' – based at RAF Cottesmore, flying the Harrier GR9. During his time on the frontline Jon was proud to support the Coalition ground forces when flying operational missions in Afghanistan. He also took part in exercises in the United Kingdom and America. As part of the Joint Force Harrier, Jon served with IV (AC) Squadron on HMS *Illustrious*, flying training missions off the UK coastline. He became the Squadron Qualified Flying Instructor during his last year on 'Happy IV', making the transition to teach on the Harrier Operational Conversion Unit, based at RAF Wittering.

Jon joined the Red Arrows in September 2010 and was selected to fly in the challenging position of Red 4. One of the highlights of this first year with the team was displaying in the Lake District in July 2011, as Jon wrote in his diary after the show:

Flt Lt Jon Egging.
(Crown Copyright/Cpl Graham Taylor)

We go full and have an awesome show. I find myself catching glimpses of the ground as we manoeuvre through the valleys, changing shapes as part of our display. I can't help but giggle as we run north up the lake for the pull into the vertical brake. As I recover over the hills that Em and I love to run over I can't help thinking what a great job I have. The only thing that could make this any better would be to have the ability to watch the show from the ground too!

Jon Egging: a remarkable man, pilot, son, husband and friend.

Dr Emma Egging

The Jon Egging Trust

It was during his time with the team, talking to the public and meeting new people, that Jon became particularly interested in combining his position as a Red Arrows' pilot and role model with his love for flying and teaching. A few weeks before his death Jon spent time in Warwickshire visiting his family. While there he made time to visit his old Air Cadet Squadron. As one cadet wrote afterwards '. . . during that evening he made us realise that we could reach for the skies'.

The Jon Egging Trust has been set up by Jon's wife Emma to realise his ambition of providing young people from disadvantaged backgrounds with new opportunities to help them achieve.

The trust's values

- To value young people, their opinions and talents
- To empower young people to be the best they can be
- To create partnerships to provide young people with new opportunities

The trust's mission

The Jon Egging Trust will use teamwork, leadership, air experience and outdoor pursuit opportunities as a practical framework to engage young people aged 13 - 25. By providing access to new opportunities the trust aims to increase young people's confidence and self esteem while providing work skills and other accredited training.

Dr Emma Egging.
(North News and Pictures)

TheJonEggingTrust
Helping young people achieve

Sean Cunningham

On 8 November 2011, Flt Lt Sean James Cunningham was tragically killed when he was ejected from his stationary aircraft at RAF Scampton. At the time of writing the cause of the accident is unknown.

Sean was born and raised in Johannesburg, South Africa, where he excelled in sports, particularly athletics, representing his city at sprints. At the age of 9, he and his family (father Jim, mother Monika and sister Nicolette) relocated to Coventry, England, where his talent for sport continued as demonstrated in him being selected to attend trials for West Bromwich Albion's Youth Team.

His dream, however, was to fly. He achieved his pilot's licence by the age of 17 after saving money from his Saturday job to pay for the numerous lessons costing £80 each. All of Sean's wages were spent on his flying lessons, demonstrating his determination and commitment to become a fast jet pilot and ultimately a Red Arrow.

On completing his A-Levels, Sean chose to read Electronic and Electrical Engineering at Nottingham Trent University where he gained a 2:1 with Honours. While at university, Sean joined the University Air Squadron in Nottingham and achieved his basic flying training for the RAF.

Sean joined the RAF in February 2000. After achieving his 'flying wings', Sean was posted to RAF Valley where he learned to fly the Hawk aircraft. Having successfully completed fast jet training, Sean was posted to RAF Lossiemouth, in Scotland where he learned to fly the Tornado aircraft. During his three years in Scotland, Sean completed several operational tours of Iraq as part of Operation TELIC, flying close air support missions for Coalition ground forces. Sean also completed a number of exercises in the USA, Canada, Romania and France.

In April 2007, Sean – now a Qualified Pilot and Tactics Instructor – began teaching newly qualified fast jet pilots to fly Tornado aircraft. He continued his instructional role when he was posted to the Weapon System Officer Training unit at RAF Leeming. This allowed him to gain further experience flying the Hawk aircraft, providing him with a greater chance of achieving his goal to join the Royal Air Force Aerobatics Team. In August 2010 Sean was successful in being selected to fly for the Red Arrows.

As a member of the Red Arrows, Sean felt that he had reached the pinnacle of his career and accomplished his dream. He had worked tirelessly to achieve his goals while never taking

⋀ **Flt Lt Sean Cunningham.**
(Crown Copyright/Cpl Graham Taylor)

anything for granted. He cherished his role and responsibility as a Red Arrow and enjoyed it immensely. He particularly enjoyed the camaraderie with his teammates, the engineers and other colleagues.

Sean was very enthusiastic and excited about his next few years in the Red Arrows. He had been given the role of training the three new Red Arrow pilots, a mentoring position which suited his fun-loving, motivational and caring personality perfectly and he relished every moment.

He will be dearly missed by all of those who knew him. He will be remembered for his easy-going nature, his love of life and his warm, infectious smile. It is hoped that Sean's approach to life, particularly his resolute determination to achieve his goals, will serve as an inspiration for others to follow.

Nicolette Cunningham

Aircraft used by Red Arrows

Folland Gnat

XM708 Although painted in Red Arrows' colours, this aircraft was a 'spare' – a standard trainer (known as a Tin Ship). It was not modified with smoke-generating equipment and had only a UHF radio. It was the unofficial 11th aircraft and belonged to 4 FTS/CFS. Transferred to No 1 School of Technical Training and allocated the maintenance serial 8573M.

XP501 Tin Ship only – see XM708. W/o 13 June 1969 when the aircraft undershot the runway at Fairford following hydraulic failure.

XP514 Withdrawn from use and sold in the USA as N7HY.

XP515 Withdrawn from use and last noted on the range at Otterburn.

XP531 W/o 16 February 1976 having been damaged beyond repair after striking a cable and making an emergency landing at Kemble.

XP533 Withdrawn from use and sold in the USA as N533XP.

XP535 Withdrawn from use and sold as G-BOXP. To N1CW. W/o 29 September 1990.

XP538 Withdrawn from use and sold in the USA as N19GT.

XP539 Tin Ship only – see XM708. W/o 22 May 1979 after aircraft was abandoned near RAF Leeming following fuel-flow problems.

XR537 Withdrawn from use and sold as G-NATY. Currently at Bournemouth.

XR540* D/d to Red Arrows, 1 February 1965. Withdrawn from use and sold in USA.

XR545 W/o 20 January 1971 when aircraft collided with XR986 while performing the Roulette manoeuvre.

XR572 Withdrawn from use and sold in the USA as N572XR.

XR573 W/o 26 March 1969. Aircraft was on loan to the Red Arrows when it flew into trees near Kemble during routine formation training flight.

XR574 Withdrawn from use and allocated 8631M. To Cosford as ground instructional airframe.

XR955 Withdrawn from use and sold in the USA as N4367L.

XR977 Withdrawn from use and allocated 8640M. Flown to Cosford 5 October 1979 for RAF Museum. Displayed in Red Arrows' colours.

XR981 W/o 3 March 1978 after aircraft struck ground while practising Vic Rollback manoeuvre at Kemble.

XR986* W/o 20 January 1971 when aircraft collided with XR545 while performing the Roulette manoeuvre.

XR987* Withdrawn from use and sold in the USA as N7CV.

XR991* Withdrawn from use and sold as G-BOXO. To N1CL.

XR992* W/o 16 December 1969 when aircraft came down in open ground close to the village of Latton, near Cirencester, after the pilot was erroneously ordered to eject having being told it had an engine fire (see XR995 below).

XR993* Withdrawn from use and sold in the USA as N3XR. W/o 9 January 1991.

XR994* W/o 13 November 1970 after aircraft suffered engine failure.

XR995* W/o 16 December 1969 when aircraft came down in open ground close to the village of Latton, near Cirencester, after an engine fire (see XR992 above).

XR996* W/o 8 October 1976.

XS101 Withdrawn from use and sold as G-GNAT. To VH-XSO, 29 October 2003.

XS107 Withdrawn from use and sold in the USA as N107XS.

XS111 W/o 8 July 1976 after aircraft suffered brake failure during landing at Kemble.

Hawk

XX156 T1 Known to be operating with the Red Arrows in 1999 and 2000. Last noted with No 4 FTS, 19(R) Squadron, RAF Valley.

XX177 T1 D/d 4 May 2010. Aircraft seriously damaged following uncommanded ejection of front seat while on the ramp at Scampton on 8 November 2011. Aircraft currently held in storage at RAF Scampton under coroner's instructions. Ultimate fate of the aircraft yet to be decided.

XX179 T1 D/d April 2002. W/o 20 August 2011 when the aircraft crashed near Bournemouth Airport after displaying on Bournemouth seafront.

XX219 T1A Expected to join the team in February 2012 – current 2012 season.

XX227 T1A D/d 14 July 1978. Aircraft is expected to be withdrawn from Red Arrows' service in mid-2012 and placed in storage.

XX233 T1 W/o 23 March 2010 after mid-air collision with XX253 over Kastelli, Crete. Other aircraft landed safely.

XX237 T1 Joined the team in 1985. Aircraft was withdrawn from Red Arrows' service and placed in storage at Shawbury on 24 October 2011.

XX241 T1 W/o 16 November 1987 when it collided with XX259 over Welton.

XX242   T1   Joined the team in 2003 from RAF Valley – current 2012 season.

XX243   T1A   W/o 22 January 1988 when aircraft crashed during low-level formation training at Scampton.

XX244   T1   Expected to join the team in March 2012 – current 2012 season.

XX245   T1   Expected to join the team in early 2012, although the aircraft is not currently fitted with the smoke generation modifications – current 2012 season.

XX251   T1   W/o 21 March 1984 when it struck the ground at Akrotiri, Cyprus.

XX252   T1A   W/o 17 November 1998 after landing short of the runway at Scampton.

XX253   T1A   Seriously damaged after mid-air collision with XX233 over Kastelli, Crete, on 23 March 2010, during formation practice. To become 'gate guard' at RAF Scampton in March 2012.

XX257   T1   W/o 31 August 1984 when it crashed at Sidmouth. Fuselage last noted at Aerospace Logistics, Charlwood, Surrey.

XX259   T1   W/o 16 November 1987 when it collided with XX241 over Welton.

XX260   T1A   Founder aircraft – joined the team in 1980. Took a bird strike and made a successful forced landing at Blackpool on Sunday, 7 August 2011. Aircraft subsequently withdrawn from use and stored at Shawbury.

XX262   T1   W/o 17 May 1980 when it hit a yacht mast at Brighton.

XX263   T1A   Expected to join the team in February 2012 although the aircraft is not currently fitted with the smoke generation modifications – current 2012 season.

XX264   T1A   Founder aircraft. Aircraft is expected to be withdrawn from Red Arrows' service by the end of the 2012 display season and placed in storage.

XX266   T1A   Founder aircraft. Aircraft is expected to be withdrawn from Red Arrows' service by the end of the 2012 display season and placed in storage.

XX284   T1A   On loan from RAF Valley. Spare aircraft, without smoke system, retains all-over black colour scheme with code CA. The aircraft has low engine life and is expected to be retired from service and placed in storage by March 2012.

XX292   T1W   Withdrawn from use and stored at Shawbury.

XX294   T1   Withdrawn from use and stored at Shawbury.

XX295   T1   Currently undergoing conversion at Shawbury in the Hawk Replacement Programme, the aircraft is expected to enter Red Arrows' service at the end of the 2012 season.

XX297   T1A   W/o 3 November 1986 when it crashed at Scampton following engine surge flameout. Allocated 8933M. To dump at Finningley.

XX304   T1A   W/o 24 June 1988 when it crashed on take-off at Scampton. To Cardiff International Airport Fire Section.

XX306   T1A   Current 2012 season.

XX307   T1   Known to be operating with the Red Arrows from 1991 to 2000. Last noted with No 4 FTS, 208(R) Squadron, RAF Valley. Retaining its all-over black gloss colours, it is to return to RAF Scampton in March 2012 to operate as the spare aircraft (replacing XX284).

XX308   T1   Joined the team in 1985 – current 2012 season.

XX311   T1   Currently undergoing conversion at Shawbury in the Hawk Replacement Programme, the aircraft is expected to enter Red Arrows' service during the middle of the 2012 season.

XX319   T1A   Joined the team in September 2011 after a major rebuild at RAF Shawbury. Previously served with FRADU at Culdrose – current 2012 season.

XX320   T1A   W/o 20 August 2008.

XX322   T1A   Joined the team in 2010 – current 2012 season.

XX323   T1A   Joined the team in October 2011 – current 2012 season.

Abbreviations

*   aircraft that served with the Yellowjacks before being repainted Post Office red at RAF Kemble during the winter overhaul, October 1964–April 1965

W/o   aircraft written off

D/d   date of delivery to the Red Arrows

Hawk Technical Specifications

	Hawk T1/T1A	Hawk 60	T-45A Goshawk	Hawk 100	Hawk 200	Hawk AJT
Dimensions						
Length (including probe)	11.85m	11.80m	11.97m	12.43m	11.35m	12.43m
Wing span (*with missiles, if appropriate)	9.39m	9.39m	9.39m	9.94m*	9.94m*	9.94m*
Wing area	16.69m²	16.69m²	16.69m²	16.69m²	16.69m²	16.69m²
Aspect ratio	5.28:1	5.28:1	5.28:1	5.28:1	5.28:1	5.28:1
Height	4.00m	4.00m	4.27m	3.99m	4.16m	3.98m
Weights and loadings						
Empty weight	3,636kg	4,012kg	4,265kg	4,400kg	4,450kg	4,440kg
Take-off weight (clean)	5,035kg			5,148kg	7,514kg	
Maximum take-off weight	5,700kg	9,100kg	5,790kg	9,100kg	9,100kg	9,100kg
Internal fuel load	1,704 lt			1,312kg	1,304kg	1,361kg
Performance						
Maximum level speed (at altitude)	560 knots/ Mach 0.9	545 Knots/ Mach 0.82	550 knots/ Mach 0.83	560 knots/ Mach 0.9	550 knots/ Mach 0.83	555 knots/ Mach 0.84
Maximum mach number	Mach 1.2	Mach 1.2	Mach 1.04	Mach 1.2	Mach 1.2	Mach 1.2
Maximum load factors	+8/-4g	+8/-4g	+7.33/-3g	+8/-4g	+8/-4g	+8/-4g
Maximum load factors (6,000lb weapons + fuel)		+6/-3g		+6/-3g	+6/-3g	+6/-3g
Maximum rate of climb at sea level	9,300ft/min		6,982ft/min	11,800ft/min	11,510ft/min	9,300ft/min
Climb to 30,000ft	6min 6secs			7min 30secs		
Take-off run (at maximum take-off weight)	1,800ft			2,100ft	5,200ft	
Landing run	1,600ft			1,980ft	1,960ft	
Standard range (without drop tanks)	1,310nm		1,000nm			1,360nm
Ferry range (includes drop tanks)	1,670nm			1,400nm	1,950nm	
Service ceiling	50,000ft		42,250ft	44,500ft	45,000ft	44,500ft
Powerplant	Adour Mk 151	Adour Mk 861	Adour Mk 871	Adour Mk 871	Adour Mk 871	Adour Mk 951
Static thrust	5,200 lb	5,700 lb	5,845 lb	5,845 lb	5,845 lb	6,500 lb

Airshow Statistics

Country	Displays	Country	Displays	Country	Displays
Australia	3	Indonesia	12	Saudi Arabia	5
Austria	9	Italy	41	Singapore	8
Bahrain	3	Jordan	14	Slovakia	4
Bangladesh	1	Libya	1	Slovenia	1
Belgium	84	Luxembourg	2	South Africa	7
Brunei	3	Malaysia	36	Spain	6
Bulgaria	1	Malta	23	Sweden	15
Canada	19	Monaco	4	Switzerland	25
Cyprus	58	Morocco	1	Thailand	3
Czech Republic	2	Netherlands	26	Turkey	10
Denmark	20	Norway	7	UAE	28
Egypt	4	Oman	5	UK	3,569
Finland	11	Pakistan	3	USA	40
France	75	Philippines	1	Zimbabwe	2
Germany	170	Poland	5		
Gibraltar	7	Portugal	3	**Total displays**	**4,410**
Greece	8	Qatar	4	**Total countries**	**54**
Hungary	1	Republic of Ireland	10		
Iceland	2	Romania	1	(As at the end of 2011 display season)	
India	5	Russia	2		

Index